KEYS TO TOILET TRAINING

Second Edition

Meg Zweiback, R.N., C.P.N.P., M.P.H.
Associate Clinical Professor of Nursing
University of California, San Francisco

BARRON'S

Cover photo © Shutterstock

DEDICATION
To Zack, Jake, and Misha

ACKNOWLEDGMENTS
Thank you to the children and parents I see every day, who are always a joy; to Myles Abbot, M.D., for suggestions, criticisms, advice, and above all, for setting high standards for children's health-care providers.

© Copyright 2009, 1998 by Barron's Educational Series, Inc.

All inquiries should be addressed to:
Barron's Educational Series, Inc.
250 Wireless Boulevard
Hauppauge, New York 11788
www.barronseduc.com

Library of Congress Control No. 2008940204

ISBN-13: 978-0-7641-4100-3
ISBN-10: 0-7641-4100-7

PRINTED IN THE UNITED STATES OF AMERICA
9 8 7 6 5 4 3 2 1

CONTENTS

Part Five—Working with Others

Part Six—Family Life

Appendix

INTRODUCTION

If you are reading this book, you are probably living with a child who is still wearing diapers. Your child may be a barely walking toddler, a lively two year old, an eager-to-learn three year old, or even a late-blooming four year old. By now, you may have been given lots of advice about toilet training from friends, family, pediatricians, child-care providers, and even your coworkers. You may be feeling confident about what is right for your child, or you may be feeling confused from hearing many different theories. You also may have heard that any mistakes you make will have long-lasting negative effects on your child, your family, and your relationships with one another.

As a pediatric nurse practitioner, I've been working with parents of young children for over 30 years. I help families who have questions about health, about behavior and development, about everyday life problems with feeding, sleep, and discipline, and about all of the many transitions that families experience. Almost every week, I meet with several families who have hit a snag during the toilet training process. I have helped so many children with toileting problems that they often call me the "poop lady!"

Even though every child, every family, every problem, and every solution is different, my clinical experience has influenced my advice to parents about toilet training difficulties in one important way. Although I have spent many years studying pediatrics and child development, I have learned that one can learn a great deal more from children and parents than from books and journals. I know that every solution to a problem has to be grounded in common sense. That is how I know for certain that parents who are generally caring and kind don't have to worry that some event during the toilet training process will cause emotional damage to their child. Children are resilient and forgiving. A single bump in the road doesn't push them off the path to emotional health. Guilt and worry drains parents, leaving them with less energy to enjoy their children. As you are reading this book, if you discover that you have taken an approach that you now wish you hadn't, or that you have dealt with a problem in a way that hasn't helped, don't look back and worry. Try something different and move on, just as you will want your children to do as they learn and grow.

Most parents will not read every key in this book all at once. It is likely that you will read the sections that seem to apply to what you are experiencing with your child at the moment. For that reason, some of the information and sugges- ˏ tions that apply to different stages and aspects of the toilet training process are included in more than one part of the book.

The advice and suggestions in the first section of this book will help you to understand your child's stage of development and how his temperamental style may influence his learning to use the toilet.

In the second section of this book, the basics of toilet training are described in depth. The approach of observing your child for signs of readiness and the gradual steps of introducing the use of the potty and the toilet are based on the work of T. Berry Brazelton, the pediatrician who first researched and published his work on child-centered toilet training: Dr. Brazelton's views have influenced many child-development professionals who give advice to parents. The details of the toilet training advice may vary. This variation is evidence that there is not a single right way to help a child become toilet trained. However, the general approach of Dr. Brazelton and those who agree with him are likely to help you and your child to be successful with the least stress and difficulty.

Even when parents wait for signs of readiness and use a relaxed, one-step-at-a-time method of toilet training, there is no guarantee that all will go easily. Sections three and four discuss common and more difficult problems. These keys describe the early signs of common problems and how parents can act to keep these problems from getting worse. Early recognition cannot always prevent children from experiencing some of the common but more complex problems of toileting, so there are also keys to help parents understand these issues and when they should seek help from the child's healthcare provider.

In the next section, concerns of working parents and the challenge of toilet training a child who is in child care is covered. Parents today are usually taking care of their children with the help of others. During the time that a child is being toilet trained, many parents will need to be involved with baby sitters, childcare providers, and extended family members who may have differing opinions. In addition, these other caretakers will also have a different kind of relationship with the child than his parents have, and this relationship may affect toilet training.

During the time you are toilet training your child, family life will continue in other ways. The events and experiences of your daily life with your child, changes in your family, and your general approach to raising your child will overlap with aspects of toilet training. In the last section, a variety of topics that are connected to toilet training and family life are discussed.

The language describing body functions and products is kept uniform throughout the book. Many adults use different words than the ones I have chosen and almost all adults will use different words when talking to a child. Language and choice of words is discussed in the key on language.

Throughout the book children are referred at times as *he* or *she* in an effort to be balanced. The word *parents* is used so that it will not be assumed that it is the mother who is the only one involved in toilet training. However, the use of the plural may imply that there are two parents in every home, which of course is not always true. Every child is different in his own way from every other child, and every family is also different in its own way from every other family. Just as parents will adapt the advice in this book to fit their child's needs, I hope that they will adapt suggestions to their family's needs.

PART ONE

HOW CHILDREN ARE DIFFERENT

1

YOUNG CHILD DEVELOPMENT

Rebecca's birthday stopped being a day to look forward to whenever I started to think about toilet training. I had planned that was when we'd begin, and somehow I felt that we didn't have a choice! After a few weeks of worrying, I realized that she didn't have to sit on the potty just because she's had a birthday cake the day before. I relaxed and decided to start when she seemed ready—which turned out to be before her birthday!

Some parents (and grandparents) are convinced that there is a right age (and a wrong age) to begin toilet training. Rebecca's mom realized that her child's chronological age wasn't as important for her to consider as her daughter's stage of development. Most child-development professionals suggest that a child who has turned two is at the best age for beginning training, but some children begin when they are younger and others when they are older. In this key you will learn about the characteristics of one, two, and three year olds. As you read about these age groups, think about how your own child compares developmentally to the children described. Do keep in mind that development often occurs in leaps and spurts, and that when a child is maturing in one area he may plateau or even slide back in another. The child you are living with today may be at a different stage next week!

One Year Olds

A one year old is a child on the move. She will progress from walking with a staggering gait at the beginning of the year to full-tilt running by her second birthday, exploring her world by moving through it.

Even though your one year old is learning to talk and respond to simple questions and directions, her learning is not primarily through words. She needs to do things, to touch things, and to order or disorder things in her own way to learn about them. "My own way" is a big concern for a one year old trying to assert her independence from her parents. She wants what she wants when she wants it, and she doesn't see the world from any point of view but her own. The one year old's activity level, need to explore and desire to please herself rather than anyone else can make toilet training a challenge this year.

However, if a parent is willing to stay in very close range, the typical one year old's love of routine can be used to advantage. A young toddler may not grasp the idea that staying dry is more fun than staying busy, but a vigilant parent may be able to "catch" a child just at the point when her stance or facial expression signals that it's "time to go." If the child is put immediately on the potty and passes urine or a bowel movement, the quick success, reinforced with praise, may create a behavioral pattern of cooperation with use of the potty. This cooperation is not the same as self-motivated and self-directed use of the toilet. A one year old will need continued parental involvement in order to stay dry. If parents don't mind making the effort, and if the one year old doesn't resist, there's no harm in trying at this stage.

Parents should remember that it is common for toddlers to become resistant or oppositional toward activities they used to love earlier in their second year. If a child is regularly using the potty and then refuses to go, parents must be prepared to step away from the battle. If parents push harder or get angry, the toddler may become more defiant. Getting into a power struggle over an issue that eventually must be the child's responsibility can lead to toilet training battles that last a long time.

Two Year Olds

By age two, most children are beginning to have a longer span of attention for quiet activities. They can sit to listen to a short story, to play with a toy, or to wait for a snack or dinner. The ability to sit and focus is very important for success in potty training.

A two year old who has routines in his daily life usually develops a sense of order and predictability. In fact, many parents will notice that some twos are so used to their routines that any change in their usual schedule is met with protests. Parents will find that a child who already has a predictable routine in other activities is more likely to cooperate with the routines of toilet training.

Many two year olds prefer order. They may line up their little cars or animal figures, put their shoes in a row, or insist that you arrange their pillows and stuffed animals just right before they go to sleep. This sense of order is an indication that they are beginning to believe that there is a "right" and "wrong" order and way to do things. This belief can be very helpful in engaging a child to master all the steps of using the potty.

A two year old's increasing ability to talk, listen, and understand will also make it possible for parents to tell or read him stories about other children being trained. His increased imagination will help to engage him in playful techniques to supplement toilet training, such as watching a doll or teddy bear use a pretend potty.

Training a two year old can also be easier for parents because even though his attention span is longer, his activities are still probably short and simple. Interrupting him to take a potty break is not as hard at this age as it will be as he matures. In addition, as the two year old's year progresses, his natural toddler negativity and oppositional behavior to whatever a parent asks tends to lessen. Nevertheless, once toilet training has begun it still works better to announce "Time to go" rather than "Do you want to go?"

Three Year Olds

A three year old is much more logical and goal oriented than a two year old. Some parents find that by waiting until a child is three, her desire to take care of herself, to take pride in her accomplishments, and to feel competent will make the toilet training process go quickly. However, waiting this long to begin training can backfire. Parents should be aware that a three year old is less willing to be distracted from play in order to use the potty. A three year old who is comfortable in diapers may feel that sitting on the potty is not nearly as interesting as finishing a puzzle or working on a drawing. In addition, a three year old is verbal enough to argue and negotiate with parents about why she doesn't want to use the potty. A younger child is still dependent enough on parents to be "trained" by a combination of parent involvement and routines that then become the child's habits. A three year old will have to be self-motivated in order to be trained, as some parents have found to their dismay.

Whether you start the toilet training process with your child at age one, two, or three will depend on what you know about your child. However, don't wait for your child to decide for you. Even though you will hear about some children who announce that they are done with diapers and are then fully trained by the next afternoon, these children are the exception. If you wait for your child to be old enough to decide for himself to use the toilet, you may be waiting for a long, long time.

2

TEMPERAMENTAL DIFFERENCES

Jerry was so easy to train that we never even thought about it being different with Katie. But she's different from her big brother in so many ways, we should have known. For one thing, she can't sit still as long as he can. And when she's angry, it's like a volcano erupting. So getting her to cooperate with sitting on the potty before she's settled down more would be impossible.

Hannah always had a long attention span and a one-track mind. The first part of potty training was easy. In fact, there were times when she wanted to sit on the potty after she was done, because she was looking at a book or examining the grout in the tile on the floor! But now that she's three and in preschool, she gets just as involved in her other activities. She won't stop playing to go to the bathroom unless the teacher tells her to go or all the other kids are going, too.

All children are different from each other at the moment they are born. We all notice the differences, and we comment on them. "He's got his dad's nose!" "That temper of hers reminds me of you!" "He loves to sit and dig in the garden—no one can believe a toddler can do one thing for so long!"

The inborn differences that parents notice among babies are called temperamental differences. These different characteristics often persist throughout a child's lifetime. Sometimes these differences can make it very challenging for a parent. This key describes some of the temperamental differences among children that can influence the course of toilet training.

Activity Level

If a child is naturally very active, a trip to the park can be a lot of fun for everyone if the park is child-proofed and fenced in. But if the very active child's parent decides to stop at the market on the way home to pick up a few things for dinner, the child may refuse to sit in the shopping cart and try to race down the aisle to get his favorite cereal. If a parent wails, "I can't take my two year old anywhere without having to chase after her at least once," the chances are that she has an active child.

An active child may be very unwilling to sit on a potty chair at an early age. Sitting isn't fun when you would much rather run! So if your child thinks a potty chair is fun to stand on to reach the sink, but you have noticed that even with a story or song she is squirming on a potty chair after a minute, it is a good idea to postpone toilet training. If parent and child engage in a struggle about sitting still, the tension will probably interfere with training and may delay cooperation even longer.

Rhythmicity

Another inborn characteristic is regularity or rhythmicity. Some babies and toddlers are very predictable in their patterns of eating, sleeping, and having bowel movements. Others are not. Parents of very regular children may find it easier to train their child because the child is already on a schedule and will be more likely to produce a bowel movement at the same time every day. In addition, parents of more regular children have usually become more routine and predictable themselves in response to their child.

Children who are less predictable allow their parents to be more flexible. They may not mind if lunch is early or a nap starts late or if every day is different than the day before. Nevertheless, a more routine schedule still has advantages when you are working on toilet training. Having predictable times and routines for daily activities help a child to learn "what happens next." It helps to look for patterns (such as having a bowel movement after a bath or wetting a new diaper right after waking up from a nap) and reinforce them whenever possible. Regular mealtimes, outdoor play, naps, and bedtime help a child and her parents to learn to tune into her body's natural rhythms.

Attention

Another characteristic of young children that affects toilet training is attention span. Children who have a longer attention span are generally easier to train. They can keep their focus on the reason they are using the potty and not turn their attention to the noises in the other room or the patterns on the wallpaper. However, the same child who can focus in on the task of using the potty also may get very involved in a puzzle, an art project, or the hole he is digging in the sandbox. Once he is involved in any activity, it is hard for him to be interrupted, and he may wet his pants without even noticing if he is engaged in something that interests him. His parents may think, "What could be more important than getting to the potty so you don't wet yourself?" To the child, nothing is as important as what he's doing right then. Parents who recognize this characteristic and accept it rather than blaming the child for having accidents will have a much easier time. As the child gets older, he can be taught to use the toilet at natural transition times, such as before going outside, so that he doesn't have to interrupt an activity.

Intensity

Another characteristic of children that can make almost any child-rearing task extra work for a parent is the quality of intensity. A very intense child is one who expresses herself passionately about everything. Parents usually do not mind when she is brimming over with laughter and delight, but when she is angry they may worry that her fury will never end. Toilet training an intense child can be a challenge because parents will have to work extra hard to stay calm and avoid battles. Although the advice throughout this book will be to avoid power struggles around toilet training, parents of intense children know that at times, everything can feel like a struggle. If an intense child is allowed to let her loud protests rule a household, she is likely to be hard to control. With intense children, it is usually better to work first on limit setting in areas other than using the toilet. Once parents have become experts at handling their passionate child's reactions at mealtime, playtime, and bedtime, they will be able to handle toilet training with more confidence and calm.

Sensitivity

Some children are very sensitive to body sensation and others are not. Children who are less sensitive often don't complain or cry when they fall down or get a bump. They may not care about the temperature of their food or notice if it is hot or cold outside. Sometimes they don't notice being hungry or thirsty. These children often don't notice the sensations of "needing to go," and they may need to be reminded to "go" for a longer time than the average child.

PART TWO

THE BASICS

3

WHEN TO BEGIN?

This book may introduce ideas about toilet training that are new to some parents. In the past, many parents began training children to use the toilet at a very early age. Mothers (not fathers!) were considered negligent if their children wore a diaper past the age of two. A big shift in our thinking about the subject occurred 40 years ago when pediatrician T. Berry Brazelton, in a study of over a thousand young children, found that with a "child-centered" approach to toilet training, most children were trained by 28 months of age, and virtually all were trained by three years. In 1997, a large study of healthy toddlers at the University of Pennsylvania School of Medicine showed a trend toward even later training, with many children, especially boys, not becoming toilet trained until after age three.

Some other factors now make it easier for parents to wait longer to begin toilet training than their parents did. Disposable diapers, diaper services, and diaper covers keep the mess and bother of changing to a minimum. In addition, most parents nowadays are "on the go" at least part of every day, so a young child is not at home all day where he can practice using the toilet in a familiar setting. Children who divide their days between home and a child-care setting make it necessary for parents to coordinate their toilet training plans with other adults who care for their child.

Family size makes a difference, too. Families are smaller than they used to be, and there are fewer big brothers and sisters for a child to learn from. Siblings are often spaced further apart in age, and parents don't worry very much about having two children in diapers at the same time.

Parents are often told, "Don't worry, he won't be in diapers when he starts kindergarten," or occasionally, "Don't worry, she won't be in diapers on her wedding day," and both statements are likely to be true. But toilet training is not a self-taught and self-motivated developmental task like learning to walk. Your child will need your assistance in learning what is expected of him and how to perform the many small activities that are part of becoming responsible for his own toileting. He will then need your supervision and support to help him continue to be responsible when he is away from home. After a while, you will both forget that he ever needed your participation, but almost all children need a parent's involvement for many months on the way to being "trained."

Since families are different in every way, they differ in the way they approach toilet training. Children are themselves different from one another, so what works with one child in a family may not work with another. What can seem like a challenge or problem during the time your child is gaining mastery of this universal task usually seems like a minor issue a few months or years later.

The key to success in toilet training is not found in starting the process at a certain age. Success follows from beginning when your child is *ready*. In the next key you will learn to recognize the signs of readiness in your child.

4

SIGNS OF READINESS

When Angela was 20 months old, we went to a family reunion. She had a ball running and climbing and playing outdoors with her older cousins. Our relatives must have asked us a dozen times, "Haven't you gotten that girl out of diapers yet?" My sister-in-law, who has five kids, shook her finger at us and said, "If I had been spending all of my time changing diapers like you, I would never have gotten anything done!" Angela's grandmother didn't seem to mind. "It's not much bother to change her, and she loves to have me help her put her clothes on when she's done. There's no rush." But we were a little upset. So when we got home, we bought a potty chair and tried to get Angela to sit down on it. But she wouldn't sit for more than ten seconds and if we urged her to sit longer she raced around the room. She was in a phase where it seemed like whatever we asked her to do she did the opposite anyway, so after a few weeks we gave up and resigned ourselves to using diapers until she was older. But we kept wondering, what are we doing wrong?

Angela's parents weren't doing anything wrong, and in all likelihood their relatives weren't either. Angela was a normal, lively toddler. Some children her age might have been ready and willing to start using the potty, especially if they had older brothers and sisters at home to imitate. But

Angela wasn't showing the signs of readiness that make toilet training go much smoother for most children.

These are the signs of readiness that will let parents know when a child is ready to begin toilet training.

- Your child is staying dry for at least two hours at a time during the day.
- You've noticed that your child is stopping briefly during play to urinate or to have a bowel movement. This tells you that your child is aware of the feelings in her body that will become her signals that its "time to go."
- Your child can understand and follow simple directions and can tell you at times that he needs to be changed (of course, that doesn't mean that he's always willing to be changed!)
- Your child is imitating lots of adult behavior, such as wanting to brush his teeth or use a fork. He's learning to undress and dress himself and tries to do things himself without help.
- Your child is able to sit still on a small chair for three to five minutes while you read or talk to her.
- Your child is not in one of the intense periods of negativity that come and go during the toddler years.

Angela, despite being a bright and verbal toddler, was not showing many of these signs of readiness. She did pause and even stand still for a moment when she was passing a bowel movement. She was dry for two to three hours at a time, but didn't give any signals that she paid any attention to the feeling of wetting or being wet. She was usually cooperative getting dressed, but she needed so much encouragement to get her to take off or put on any clothing by herself that her parents did most of the changing themselves. Angela loved to run and play, and could keep up with the older children's racing about. But she wasn't very interested in sitting quietly. In fact, her parents had noticed that until very recently she liked to walk around while they read to her at bedtime. It was only since she had started to enjoy looking at pictures in the books and pointing to different objects that she was willing to sit down for more than five minutes. Last, Angela was starting to be oppositional in her daily interactions with her parents. Like many toddlers, she was asserting her independence by saying "no" even when she seemed to want to say yes and doing almost anything except what her parents had just asked her to do. If Angela's parents had persisted in trying to get her to use the potty, that oppositional behavior, added to the areas in which she was not developmentally ready to be successful in toileting, would have turned the experience into an unnecessary battle.

Instead, Angela's parents stopped coaxing her to sit on the potty. They called their relatives for tips on what had and hadn't worked for them. To their surprise, they found out that although some of the cousins had started to use the toilet before they were two years old, others hadn't even been willing to sit on the potty until they were two-and-a-half. The tips were so varied that Angela's parents realized that there was no uniform technique that was likely to work for their daughter or any other child, and that the general advice to "Get started now" didn't have to be taken as anything more than a suggestion.

5

GETTING STARTED: STAGE ONE

After your child seems ready for beginning toilet training, the next step toward success is to make sure that parents are ready, too. Before you start, wait for a time when your life can be fairly routine and stable for several weeks, if not longer. Don't plan to begin training if the family is experiencing a disruption such as illness, difficulty between parents, or severe emotional distress. The birth of a new baby is discussed in a separate section. Although you would not want to introduce toilet training along with a new baby, there is no reason to wait until after a baby is born if your older child seems ready a month or two before the baby is due.

Avoid starting training during times of family upheaval. That doesn't mean that you must wait until there are no changes or stresses at all in your family. However, since training requires your child to learn new patterns, it's best if he doesn't have to adapt his learning in a variety of settings, at irregular hours, or with many different people. Children who have to cope with lots of unpredictability in daily life sometimes have difficulty adapting to new routines. Even if a child is "ready" developmentally, it will be easier for him to learn if he is in a situation that is supportive of his practicing new skills with regularity. If life is unpredictable at present, you may want to delay toilet training until your child is older. You may also want to think about bringing more structure into your lives.

Some busy families have successfully begun training children while on vacation. Even though a vacation setting is less familiar than home, the family is relaxed and moving at a slower pace than usual.

If you and your child are ready to start, now is the time to purchase a potty chair if you haven't done so already. If you've had a chair since your child was younger and smaller, make sure that it is still a comfortable size. It's important that your child be comfortable in the seat and that the chair be the right size for him to be able to rest his feet on a hard surface while he is "going." More information about potty chairs can be found in Key 7, "Choosing a Potty." Tell your child, "This is your potty," and let him examine it, carry it, take it apart, and decide with you where it should be placed.

For many children, especially young two year olds, it's best to begin by letting your child practice using the chair while he's dressed. The potty seat can feel cold and hard at first, so having cloth between skin and chair is easier for many children. Of course, if your child wants to take his diaper off, that's fine.

Bring a favorite teddy bear or doll in to "watch." You can let the teddy or doll have a chance to try sitting, too. Imaginative parents can talk about how the doll feels very pleased with the new potty, or about how Teddy has been hoping for some time to have a potty of his own. Most children love to watch a teddy bear or doll "sit" and you can continue to use this technique to model all of the other toileting behaviors you'll be teaching. Young children learn much more by watching than by having a parent tell them what to do.

Have your child "sit" for a few minutes while you read him a story, sing a song, or just chat. Tell him that he's practicing sitting on the potty now, and that after awhile he'll be able to use the potty when it's time to "pee" or "poop" or whatever words you choose to use. If he doesn't want to sit, don't try to persuade him. If a child is resistant to sitting at all and a parent insists, a power struggle will begin that can delay the entire process. Continue this practicing for a few days or a week.

In the second week, at a time when your child is undressed such as before or after his bath, suggest to your child that he try sitting on the potty bare bottomed. Again, don't insist that your child sit if he doesn't want to. Continue your practice sessions once or at most twice a day for about another week. At this point, your child will be comfortable with the potty as something that is familiar and a part of his daily routine. He may have added on his own routines, such as taking the potty around the house with him or pretending to read a story while his teddy bear sits. Your child is now ready to have more practice times that can be geared toward him actually using the potty to "go."

6

GETTING STARTED:
STAGE TWO

Once your child is happy to sit on his potty chair for a few minutes every day, you can begin to increase his opportunities to practice. The toilet training steps described in this key can best be called a one-step-at-a-time plan. Each step builds on the one before. As parent and child practice each step, the emphasis is on cooperation, not on pushing the child. Because the pace is slow and the amount of time spent each day practicing is brief, most children will enjoy the activity of "sitting." If the child resists more than a small amount, the parent eases up any pressure or takes a break from the process. The training plan is designed to achieve slow, steady, progress toward independent toilet training. Some children may become trained quickly, but the goal of this method is not speedy training. The goal is a child who is independent and proud of his accomplishment.

If your child is willing, you can now start to have him sit on his potty chair at more regular times. Always choose a relaxed time for having him sit. After meals, the middle of the morning, or right after a nap, or before or after a bath are times that usually work well. Whatever time you choose, your child must feel that it is easy and pleasant to sit on the potty. You don't have to make it the most exciting or important part of his day.

Some children like to sit on a potty while watching a parent get ready for the day in front of the bathroom sink. If parents feel comfortable, they can allow the child to watch them while they sit on the toilet. The child may even want to sit on his potty chair at the same time. Even if fathers want to show their sons how they urinate standing up, it is wise to encourage boys to sit at first. A little boy can be taught how to push his penis down to direct the stream of urine into the potty or toilet. It takes a while for little boys to learn to aim and it is best to master use of the potty sitting down before teaching another skill.

Keep up this pattern of regular times to sit, but don't put pressure on your child. If she is unwilling to sit very often, take a break for a week or two and then try again. Keep each session brief. Always choose a time when your child is not too involved with something else. When you take her to the potty, help her take her diaper off and look to see if it is wet or has a bowel movement in it. You can say, "Look, someday you'll be putting your poop and pee in the potty chair instead of in your diaper."

When you want your child to go sit on the potty chair, don't ask, "Would you like to use the potty?" A two year old often answers all questions with "No!" Instead say very matter-of-factly, "Let's go use the potty now," or "This would be a good time to sit on the potty while I read you a story." If your child is still reluctant, ease up on the requests or stop them altogether for a few weeks.

Some parents are able to choose times when they've noticed that their child usually passes urine or a bowel movement. In this way they increase the chance that their child will "go" while he's sitting. If your child wakes up dry from a nap or in the morning, there is an excellent chance he will need to go soon. After a meal, the feeling of fullness in a child's abdomen triggers a natural reflex that may cause him to move his bowels. While your child is sitting, stay with him, just talking or reading a short story. Remember to keep the time for each sitting short, not more than two to three minutes, and don't coax or force your child to sit if he doesn't want to.

At some point in this process, perhaps right away or perhaps after several weeks, your child will pass urine or a bowel movement into the potty. This moment is, of course, the moment that parents have been awaiting. It is tempting to respond to the event as the most wonderful accomplishment ever. Many parents are so thrilled that they shower the child with praise. For some children, this reaction increases their pleasure and may motivate them to try for more successes. However, sometimes too much of a celebration can overwhelm a child. You don't want your own excitement at this achievement to be more of a motivation than the child's own pride in his accomplishment.

After your child has had a success, suggest that when he is done he look to see what he has put into the potty each time he sits. There will, of course, be times when he has not put anything in. When that is the case, say "Oh well, another time there will be something to see again." When he produces something, tell him that the next step is that you are going to put it in the toilet. Remind him that you flush your own pee and poop down the toilet when you go to the bathroom. You can ask him if he wants to watch, and whether he wants to flush the toilet himself. Some children are very interested in watching things go down the toilet and may love to be in charge of flushing. Some children may seem upset by watching you flush away what they've just produced. If your child seems bothered by the flushing, skip that step until he leaves the room.

It usually doesn't help to explain to a two-year-old or young three-year-old child how the toilet works. As children get to be three and a half or four years old, they tend to become more interested in the plumbing. However, you can point to the hole in the toilet and tell your child that it is small, just the right size for a bit of poop and some toilet paper, but not for much else. If your child does like to watch the toilet flush, make sure to let him know that the toilet is not a toy. Tell him that he can only use the toilet when you are with him. If your child tends to like to experiment, you may need to put a safety hook on the toilet lid and store toilet paper out of reach in order to avoid a visit from the plumber.

Once your child has used the potty successfully once, you will probably be hoping that he'll begin using it every time. He might, but he might not. If he is cooperative, you can increase the number of times a day you take him to the potty. If you are at home all day, you can suggest going to the potty about every two to three hours.

Continue to keep each sitting time brief. If your child wants to sit longer that three minutes, you don't have to remove him, but don't encourage long sitting by continuing to read or talk. You don't want to teach him that potty time is social time.

Even if you notice that your child tends to wet or have a bowel movement in his diaper five minutes after he gets up, don't try to make him sit longer. He may not be aware enough yet of the sensation of "needing to go" to be able to get back to the potty. He also may have wanted to wait until he had his diaper back on to let go. If you make him sit longer, he may start to hold on rather than to gradually get comfortable enough to let go. It won't help to get angry at your child for going later. It may hurt his progress if he feels that you are trying to be in charge of his body. Most two year olds will respond to that kind of pressure by resisting. Instead of scolding or expressing disappointment, change the diaper and tell your child that someday soon he'll be able to use the potty instead of the diaper all by himself.

Continue with this stage of training until your child is urinating or having a bowel movement in the potty several times a day. You can help your child by keeping clothing simple and having him wear pants that are easy to pull down quickly. Some parents find that it is helpful to also allow the child to play around the house without a diaper on so that the child can also initiate getting to the potty quickly if he has the urge to go. The advantage to this method is the child may feel the desire to go and be able to reach his potty chair quickly without having to remove clothing. If he gets to the potty in time, he is more likely to be successful and to have the feelings of satisfaction that go along with success.

This method can work very well if parents don't mind cleaning up puddles. However, most children are not in situations throughout the day where being half-dressed is practical, so most children will stay in diapers during this early stage of training. It may be days, weeks, or months before a child begins to put his urine or bowel movements in the potty more often than he puts them in his diapers. That's why it's important to keep the sitting time short. You won't be spending more than ten to fifteen minutes a day total in this activity, but your child will be learning at his own pace.

Once your child gets to the point of sitting on the potty several times a day and is able to produce urine or a bowel movement more than half of the time he goes, it is time to introduce padded training pants or cloth underpants for him to wear during the day. Some people think that it is better to take diapers away before that time so the child will be motivated by feeling cold or wet if he goes in his pants. Key 8, "Diaper/Training Pants/Underwear—What's Best?," discusses this choice in detail.

It's possible that the feeling of being cold and wet will motivate your child, but many children don't notice or care. If you decide to try taking away the diapers when your child is still regularly wetting them, don't make a fuss about it. Tell him you're just going to try the cloth pants for a few days and see how it goes. If your child continues to go in his pants instead of the potty, it will of course be more work for you to clean up. It can be hard to be cheerful about cleaning up messy pants for weeks at a time, especially if your child doesn't seem to care. Some parents find that if they begin using cloth pants too soon they wind up getting very angry and even losing their temper at their child. Although a child may react to parents' anger by trying harder to stay dry, he is just as likely to react by being more unwilling to go into the potty.

Once you do take your child out of diapers, he will need to be reminded to sit in the potty at regular, frequent intervals. Some children will go on their own, but it's reasonable to think that the parent may need to offer a casual reminder every two hours or so. Set a timer or ring a bell so that the buzzer or bell "tells" the child to go, rather than the parent. Don't watch the clock. The purpose of the reminders is to help the child have the feeling of being successful more often, not to avoid having any accidents. If you have to urge your child to go or if he resists a reminder or a bell, it's best to let him go at his own pace, even if it means more puddles.

Every time your child tries or succeeds on the potty, offer him mild praise. Just as it was at the start of training, your goal is to let him know that you have noticed his accomplishment and to allow him to feel that using the potty or toilet is evidence of how competent he is. If you go overboard with praise and congratulations, he will start using the toilet just to please you, or worse, refuse to use the toilet to show you that he's the boss of his body.

Slow, steady progress toward independent toileting takes less time in the long run. Some training plans push the child so quickly that parents wind up having to back off repeatedly from their efforts. One child may take several months to get through the steps above, but another may go from simple sitting to training pants in a few weeks and be mostly accident-free after a month or two. Success is achieved at the child's pace, but the success is likely to last.

7

CHOOSING A POTTY

We knew that Austin was getting ready to start using the potty when we saw him watching intently when his little friend Jordan sat on the potty. Jordan lives next door. He's six months older than our son, and Austin worships him. So it seemed like a good idea to get Austin the same kind of potty chair that Jordan was using. He was thrilled, and I'm sure that's why he was so easy to train.

Not all parents are lucky enough to have a next-door-neighbor to model potty chair use. Austin's story illustrates how the choice of a potty chair is less about which model is "right" than which model is the one that your child will want to use.

There are a number of advantages to beginning toilet training a child by using a potty chair rather than an adult-size toilet. The most important advantage of a potty chair is that it is sized for a small child's height and bottom size. Children tend to like child-sized furniture. When your child is getting used to sitting, whether with clothing on or a bare bottom, having a potty that is just her size can make the transition out of diapers easier.

In addition, the potty is close to the floor, which makes it possible for a child's feet to be flat on the floor. It is much easier to have control of pushing out a bowel movement if you can press down with your feet at the same time. Imagine how you would feel if you tried to have a bowel movement while your feet were dangling in the air!

Using the potty chair also provides a child with the opportunity to be more independent. Although many children will want a parent close by in the early stages of training, once a child has mastered the steps of getting to the potty she will need less help if she doesn't need a boost up or someone to adjust her step stool. If there are more people than toilets in the house, it also makes it possible for the child to take her time without a line forming for use of the big toilet.

When a child eliminates into a potty, she can see what she's produced. For some children this is highly desirable. However, if your child is reluctant to dispose of her product, it is fine for parents to let the child leave and to then flush the contents into the toilet. Some children love to be a part of these final steps, wanting to push down the toilet handle themselves and even waving good-bye to their output as it disappears. Others, especially two year olds, prefer to leave their prize for the adults to tend to.

Cleaning the potty chair should not be a child's task. The child will learn nothing useful from doing so and it is too easy for this job to become an area of struggle rather than of cooperation.

Some parents like the portability of the potty chair. It can go inside, outside, to the park, or on a family trip. The portability is a definite advantage. The one disadvantage is that the child can start feeling as though her potty should come to her rather than her having to go to it. During the early stages of training, when a child can barely get to the potty in time, it is very helpful to have the potty close by. But once a child is in underpants most of the time or seems to be able to hold on longer, try to keep the potty chair in the bathroom as much as you can. If you are having your child sit for a few minutes after meals in order to produce a bowel movement, the bathroom will provide her with privacy and will make the rest of the family more comfortable as well. Over time you want your child to understand that "going to the bathroom" is the way that children eliminate as they get older.

In choosing a potty chair, look for features that will be comfortable for your child and make cleaning up easier for you. Sturdy legs that do not skid, a comfortable seat that allows for room to grow, and a bowl that is easy to remove for cleaning are essential features. Many potty chairs have "deflectors" designed to keep a little boy from splashing urine on the seat or floor. They are often not helpful and have the disadvantage of catching on a child as he sits down. It is better to teach a little boy to push his penis down when he urinates so that he doesn't spray the floor or walls.

Some potty chairs have safety straps, but a child who cannot sit safely on the potty without a strap is not old enough to be sitting there at all. A safety strap should never be used to keep a child sitting longer than he is willing to sit. All of the other potty and toilet gimmicks such as music boxes, cartoon characters, targets for boys to aim at, and fancy look-like-the-big-toilet models may appeal to you or your child, but are not necessary. As much as parents may hope that fancy accessories will make toilet training easier, it will be a child's readiness and willingness that determines how quickly the process will go.

Does you child need a potty chair at all? Some parents skip the stage of potty chair use and go directly to the toilet, using an adapter, an insert that makes the toilet seat smaller.

Since some chairs can be converted to be used later as adapters, you can begin with one method and change later. If your child begins using an adapter on a regular toilet, you should provide her with a step stool to keep beneath her feet to press down on, even if she can climb onto the toilet by herself.

Some children may want to try to sit on the big toilet while a parent holds their hands for balance, but this approach will make for more work for the parent. In addition, even if a child can balance, the effort is likely to contribute to her tensing her muscles. This tension can make it very difficult for her to relax enough to fully empty her bladder or pass a bowel movement.

Once a child is out of diapers all the time, it is a good idea to practice a little with balancing on the big toilet so that if you are ever somewhere where your child cannot get to a potty, she has had some experience. (In an emergency, a child can sit facing the back of a big toilet so that her bottom is completely supported by the toilet seat.) Even if a child has mastered potty sitting well, it can be hard to use a toilet without practice. It's a good idea for parents to carry a change of clothing for the child who winds up having an accident while trying to go on a big toilet.

8

DIAPERS/TRAINING PANTS/UNDERWEAR— WHAT'S BEST?

As soon as Madeline was in underwear and made her first puddle, it all seemed to click for her. She almost always made it to the potty after that.

Justin wanted regular underpants, but he had lots of accidents when he wore them. Using training pants was a compromise we could all live with.

I couldn't deal with training pants or underwear until Shana had her bowel movements under control. They were unpredictable and soft and I knew my irritation at having to clean up was affecting my reactions to her.

I felt guilty about using disposables all the time, but I decided to stick with the convenience and increase my recycling of other stuff! Everyone said it would take longer to train Peter, but he was out of diapers and accident-free before some of his friends who were wearing cloth!

Parents will be given many different opinions abut when to take a child out of diapers and what the next step should be. The choice of diapers, pull-ups, training pants, or underwear is best made by looking at the practicalities of each, based on where the child is in the process of training. Parents who are not overburdened by clean-up are much more likely to be relaxed and patient with a child who needs time before she can be accident-free.

Changes in toilet raining expectations have led to children wearing diapers for many months longer than they did in the past. Manufacturers of disposable diapers have helped this trend by producing diapers that absorb large amounts of liquid and that are available in sizes that fit older children. These highly absorbent diapers don't have to be changed as often as cloth diapers because children often don't notice the discomfort of wetness that helps them connect the body sensations that precede elimination. The price of this convenience to parents of less frequent changing is high. Disposable diapers are much more expensive than cloth diapers laundered by a professional diaper service. Perhaps even more costly is the damage to the environment as this waste is added to landfills all over the planet. Although the use of disposable diapers has become the norm for most families, especially if children are in child care, it is worthwhile considering the use of cloth as well.

For some children, the motivation of pretty panties or super hero briefs is the trigger for becoming trained, often very quickly. Unfortunately, many children beg for underwear, are thrilled to wear it, and may even stay dry for the first exciting days of wearing it until they lose interest and begin to wet their pants almost as often as if they were in diapers.

Most children stay in diapers until parents notice that they are staying accident-free at least part of the time when they are at home. Although some people say that the uncomfortable wetness of thick cloth training pants motivates children more than the superabsorbent disposable diapers, many parents haven't found that to be true. A child who isn't sensitive to wetness may ignore the feeling of wet cloth, even cold, wet cloth. Sometimes parents of a child who gets painful diaper rashes are counseled to train their child early to avoid the irritation of wet diapers against inflamed skin. Even in those circumstances, parents find the child doesn't understand that using a potty will make his bottom hurt less.

It is a good idea for parents to continue with the type of cloth or disposable diaper that has been most convenient until your child is partly trained. Many parents will want to wait even longer, until the child is using the potty or toilet most of the time. Once the decision is made to discontinue diapers, the choice is among cloth training pants, disposable pull-ups that a child can manage without parents' help, or regular underwear.

Training pants have the advantage of being absorbent of accidents, but having the look of real underpants. If a child wets or has a bowel movement, the training pant may be able to keep the contents of the accident in place until the child can be changed. Most children will object to the feeling of a full or wet training pant if they are already using the potty or toilet most of the time. Training pants are economical because they are reusable, but some parents find that it is difficult to wash and dry soiled pants and prefer the disposables. If training pants have to be removed, the child will have to undress from the waist down and if the pants are soiled, he will probably have to take shoes and socks off, too.

Some parents prefer to use the thinner *disposable pull-ups* as the first step away from diapers. The advantage of pull-ups can be that a child can easily pull them down along with his clothing and use the potty, but clothing and floors are protected from accidents. However, the absorbency of the pull-up will keep the child from noticing that he is wet. If a child is not yet motivated to use the potty, pull-ups may make him even less so. Pull-ups are much more expensive than training pants, so most parents will not want to use them until a child is almost trained. Pull-ups are also more expensive than diapers, so most parents will not want to use them if the child needs frequent changes.

The privilege of wearing *real underwear* is a sign to most children that they are getting "big." For boys, especially, the thrill of super heroes on briefs is very special. Some boys will prefer to wear their briefs backward at first because the rear designs are often more elaborate. For girls, the choice of designs and colors is more varied. Of course, both boys and girls can wear less expensive plain underwear and still be successful in using the toilet.

The Transition

When you make the transition, begin first at home. You can continue to allow or require your child to wear more protection on outings where it might be hard to get to a potty quickly. If your child is very late in training, pull-ups can be used during the day even before the partial training point if you want him to look less like a "baby" in diapers and so he doesn't need as much help from you to use the potty.

During warm weather, some parents will let a child go without diapers and underwear. For some children, being undressed helps them to connect the feeling of needing to go with the action of going. However, some children will make lots of puddles around the house. Parents shouldn't try this method if they will be upset about mopping up floors, rugs, and furniture or if they have floor coverings that can stain.

Some parents try to motivate their child by saying, "Don't you want to be like your friends?" or "If the other kids find out you're in diapers, they might tease you." While this approach may work for some, it has the side effect of supporting the attitude of "do what the other kids are doing." This attitude can backfire in a few years. Many parents welcome the idea of peer pressure when it comes to the idea of a child being toilet trained but feel differently when the pressure is to wear "cool" clothing or stay up late "because everyone else is doing it."

Parents should be cautious about making the transition to underwear if it is not clear that a child is mostly trained. That will decrease the chances of having to return to diapers if a child doesn't meet expectations. It is usually best if a child is told, "You've been doing a great job of getting to the potty. I think you're ready to wear underwear now." That is better than saying, "Now you're a big boy and there aren't going to be any more diapers." The wearing of underwear is then linked to the behavior of the child rather than to his being bigger and older. That leaves room for you to have your child wear diapers in situations where it might be difficult for him to get to a toilet. Once you switch to underwear, if your child doesn't continue to make progress or regresses, avoid telling him, "If you can't stay dry you're going to have to wear diapers again." A return to diapers for any reason can wind up feeling like a punishment rather than as a practical solution for a child who is not able to stay dry.

Three-year-old Caroline had been out of diapers for almost a year, but hardly ever made it to the bathroom. Her parents were often very angry at her, but they were afraid to tell her she had to wear diapers because they thought that would hold her back even more. Her parents finally realized that the tension and arguments about her accidents might be worse than going back to diapers. They told Caroline that it was too much work for them for her to be in underpants. They didn't want to keep being angry—Caroline was well aware of their anger—and they wanted her to be in diapers until she was ready to stay dry most of the time. Caroline acted very angry at first and even tore her diaper off a few times. Her parents stayed calm and put it back on her after each tantrum. Once Caroline saw that they had disengaged from the battle, she was able to calm down too.

For a month, Caroline stayed in diapers and acted as if she had never been out of them. Then one day she started announcing that she had to go. After another month she was making it to the potty about half the time, but her parents decided to move slowly. One more month passed, and Caroline made it to the potty for almost all of her peeing and some of her bowel movements, which were usually in the evening. Caroline's parents suggested that she start wearing underpants again, but after dinner she could put on a diaper so that she didn't have to worry about getting to the bathroom. Caroline agreed, but a week later she said she didn't want her diaper on in the evening either. She rarely had an accident again.

9
DIET

Ian was always such a fussy eater that we let him drink as much milk as he wanted. He looked healthy and he gained weight fine, but he just picked at his food. Then he started having hard bowel movements and telling us that they hurt. Everyone said to give him more foods with fiber, but he wasn't interested. Finally, we realized that he drank so much milk that he was never hungry for the foods that might loosen him up. Once we cut back on the milk he had enough room to eat other foods.

Most preschool-age children have favorite foods that they prefer to eat over and over again. Parents may try to introduce a wider variety of tastes and textures, but children don't always cooperate. Parents may tell resistant children that some foods are "good for them" or "help them grow big and strong," but these explanations don't usually motivate a preschool-age child to choose one food over another. The best approach to feeding children is to offer them a variety of simply prepared foods and let them choose how much of each one to eat. However, as Ian's parents discovered, even a food that is healthy and well-liked by a child can crowd out other healthy foods if quantities aren't limited. Dairy products are a good source of calcium and protein, and most children enjoy drinking milk. A few children love to drink milk so much that they request it at every meal and throughout the day. They may drink far more than the pint of milk they need daily to help them build strong bones. Some three year olds would be happy to drink a quart of milk a day. They are not hungry at mealtime and often refuse to eat the fruits, vegetables, protein-rich foods, and grains they need. In addition, they may crowd out the foods that have the fiber that helps bowel movements to be soft.

Some children have a tendency to produce hard or small bowel movements unless they eat fruits, juices, and fiber-rich grains every day. Some parents may have noticed this tendency ever since the child started eating solid foods. The toddler's natural decrease in appetite and fussiness about foods can lead to food choices that don't have the fiber that will help the bowel movements to be softer, larger, and easier to pass.

Ian's parents realized that all of the milk he was drinking left him no appetite for other foods. They had to limit milk and also limit his other food choices to foods they knew would help his bowel movements. Milk is one food that in excess can cause hard bowel movements, but other foods may need to be limited as well.

Certain foods tend to make bowel movements harder. Milk and cheese in excess produce a common problem. Other foods that are popular with young children but may have to be limited are white rice, white bread, bananas, and applesauce. The children who are most likely to have difficulties are those who fill up on snack foods, such as crackers or sweets. Snacks and sweets in small quantities aren't harmful, but many children eat these foods throughout the day and wind up being overweight and undernourished. It can be hard to change habits learned in early childhood, so the best way to help your child to have good eating habits is to start young.

In addition to eating a variety of nutritious foods, everyone needs to eat foods that have fiber. Fiber is the part of food that is not absorbed by the body during digestion. Instead, it passes through the body and helps to push the bowel movement through. More fiber tends to make it easier to pass soft bowel movements.

Foods that will make bowel movements softer are

- Fruits with seeds or lots of skin, such as berries, grapes, plums, and apricots
- Dried fruits, especially prunes
- Prune juice
- Pear nectar
- Brown rice
- Breads made with whole wheat flour
- Cereals with bran
- Any baked products with bran mixed in
- Lots of water

However, too much fiber can give a child or an adult cramps or gas, so don't overdo it. Introduce high fiber gradually, and make sure that your child is drinking plenty of liquid.

All young children should be offered a well-balanced choice of foods every day. Many children will not want to try a new food until it has been presented many times. It's important to avoid battles over food, but you don't have to be a short-order cook either. If snacks and sweets are limited, most children will have the appetite for at least some of the foods they should eat each day.

Here is what your child needs each day:

- Two servings of milk. A serving is 1 cup of milk or 1 ounce of cheese.
- Two servings of protein rich foods. A serving is 2 to 3 ounces of meat, fish, or poultry; 1/2 cup of cooked beans; 1 egg; or 2 tablespoons of peanut butter.
- Three servings of vegetables. A serving is 1/2 cup of raw or cooked vegetables.

- Two servings of fruit. A serving is a 1/2 cup of fruit or 3/4 cup of juice.
- Six servings of grains. A serving is 1 slice of bread; 1/2 cup of rice, pasta, or cooked cereal; or 1 ounce of cold cereal.

Some children won't want to eat this much food, even if snacks and sweets are limited. As long as a child is growing well, there's no need to worry. However, a child who refuses milk should be given a calcium/vitamin D supplement, and a child who pushes away vegetables and fruits should be given a multivitamin. With this well-balanced diet, most children will be able to have regular, soft bowel movements, even if they prefer to eat macaroni and cheese rather than whole grain breads or bananas rather than blueberries.

10
REWARDS AND CHARTS

My husband promised Kevin that if he would start using the potty he'd get him a really elaborate train set. We bought the set and it's been sitting in the hall closet. I think Kevin feels bad every time he sees it, and I know he would love to have it, but it doesn't help him stay dry.

―――――――――

Alexis loved the stickers so much she'd tell me she had to go, make two drops and say, "I'm done." In between her trips to the potty for stickers, she wet her underwear half the time. We finally dropped the whole idea.

―――――――――

Anna's grandmother said she'd give her a doll if she could stay dry all week. She'd never gone for more than two days without an accident before, but she did it. I think that having the doll reminded her of what she could do if she really tried, and she stayed dry a lot more after that. But she still had accidents for another few months.

Many parents think that the key to successful toilet training is finding the right prize that will motivate their child to train himself. Almost everyone knows someone who told a child, "As soon as you start using the toilet, we'll take you to Disneyland," and by the next afternoon the child was fully trained and standing by the front door with his suitcase packed. It is true that rewards and prizes can help some children take the final step toward independent toileting. But the child who is at the beginning stages of toilet training probably will not have the ability to become trained just in response to a promised reward.

The method of early toilet training described in this book includes providing a very important reward: positive attention from the parent. The parent is encouraged to make every trip to the potty pleasant so that each time the child is taken to "go" his associations with the experience are positive. The parent is urged to avoid pushing the child who is in a negative mood so that the child does not learn to associate going to the potty with a power struggle.

After a child is using the potty frequently, an extra method of noting or rewarding using the potty can be helpful. There are a number of different methods that parents can use to reinforce success. Some tend to work better than others, depending on the child.

- Charts: A chart helps the child and parent to record successes for any type of behavior. The child or parent places a check or a sticker on the chart every time the child accomplishes the chosen task. Charts work best when they help a child to feel proud of his accomplishments, so the tasks must be ones that a child is able to complete at least some of the time. A chart that is filled with empty spaces is not very encouraging. For example, if the child is using the potty some of the time, but going in his diaper at other times, he might get a star for every time he goes to the potty. If he is in underwear already, he might get a star for every time he goes to the potty without being reminded. He might also get a sticker for staying dry all day.

Sometimes parents want to use a chart to mark progress for several days of success. For example, the child may get a treat, a present, or an activity with a parent if he goes a week without an accident. However, if a reward is days or weeks away, most young children cannot sustain motivation. In addition, if a child has a day that interrupts his progress toward a reward and he has to start over, he may just give up.

When parents use a chart to monitor toilet training progress it is helpful to add another chart to notice other positive behavior. Getting dressed by himself, picking up toys, or getting in and out of the bath when asked are the type of tasks that can be charted along with using the potty.

- Promises: Most parents will try using promises to motivate a child. "We can go to the toy store on the way home if you promise to use the toilet all afternoon." "If I let you wear your party dress without a diaper you have to promise me you won't have an accident." Unfortunately, it usually does not work to ask a young child to stick to a promise in exchange for something she wants. A preschool-age child only understands the feelings, wants, and desires she is experiencing in the present. She can promise a parent anything, but she should not be expected, at her age, to keep a promise, no matter what she says. A preschool-age child should never be punished or penalized for saying she will do something later and then refusing because the parent should not ask for the promise in the first place.

- Rewards and Treats: Some children, especially older twos and threes can be tempted to sit on the potty or use the potty more easily if they are offered a treat. Stickers, sweets, or even small prizes may work well if a child is developmentally and emotionally ready to be toilet trained anyway. The treats are a reinforcement of the behavior and motivate a child to keep practicing. Parents sometimes begin by offering a treat for sitting on the potty, but then cut back to only offering a treat if the child actually produces something. Otherwise some children will run to the potty every half hour and sit for a few minutes just to get another cookie.

11

KEEPING CLEAN

When Jennifer was learning to use the potty she would be very happy to sit anywhere, anytime. Sometimes she'd go, sometimes she wouldn't, but she never had to be urged at all. When she was done, though, there was always a fuss. She needed our help in getting off, getting cleaned up, getting dressed again, everything. One evening her dad came home and heard her calling from the bathroom, "Daddy, Daddy, come here now!" He went in and found her grinning up at him. "Look Daddy, I'm the pooper and you're the wiper!"

P arents would like it very much if a child could master all aspects of using the potty and the toilet independently right away. Cleaning up after a child who is using the potty and teaching her to participate in her own care is as much work for a while as changing diapers. Parents can make it easier for a child to learn good habits of cleanliness and hygiene, but they will have to participate and supervise for quite a while.

Even before your child begins toilet training, it is important for your family's health that the adults follow a routine around bathroom use that can be taught to a child as she gets older. You probably learned when your child was an infant that in order to keep the work of diapering to a minimum you had to be well organized with all of your equipment. The same is true when you introduce a potty chair.

The best way to keep your child and your family healthy is for everyone to wash hands well, especially after every use of the toilet and before touching or eating food. Washing hands well after using the bathroom prevents the spread of viruses and bacteria that are left on hands after you wipe yourself. If hands are not washed well, the viruses and bacteria multiply and can be left on other surfaces to grow. That is why we tell children to wash their hands even when they protest that their hands don't have any dirt on them. Washing hands well means wetting them thoroughly, then using soap and washing for 20 seconds. Teach your child to wash while singing "Row, Row Your Boat" or "Twinkle Twinkle Little Star."

To make handwashing easier, it's best to keep soap at every sink. Most children like using liquid soap that they can easily pump on their hands. Anti-bacterial soaps should be avoided because over time, they promote resistant strains of bacteria. Alcohol-based hand sanitizers are also safe and effective, unless hands have dirt on them. Cloth towels are fine if they are washed frequently, but if they are used over and over by everyone in the family, they are not as safe as paper towels. It will be easier for a child to cooperate with handwashing if you keep a small stool in front of the sink so that she doesn't have to stretch. Once she is sitting on the toilet, she can use the same stool to help her stay balanced and able to push down.

Once your child is going into the potty or toilet, it is time to teach wiping. A little boy can just "shake" dry after urinating, but a little girl should be taught to wipe herself from front to back. This will prevent bacteria from the skin folds or rectal area from getting into the urethra, where it can cause a urinary tract infection. The urethra is the small tube that leads from the urinary bladder to the outside.

Most children will need to have their bottoms wiped by an adult until they are about four years old. After that you can share the responsibility with them. It usually works well to have the parent do the first wipe, the child the second, and to take turns until the child can do the last wipe and be all clean. Some children find it easier to use a premoistened baby wipe while they are learning. Again, girls should be taught to wipe from front to back. If you have a full length mirror or a hand mirror in the bathroom, your child can check herself and tell you when she is clean, which is an excellent way to help her to assume total responsibility eventually. You can also teach your child to wipe until the last piece of tissue is clean.

After wiping, always make sure that your child discards toilet tissue into the toilet and flushes or has you flush. Remind your child that the hole in the toilet is small, and that not very much can go through it or it will clog up. This explanation provides an indirect reassurance to the child that he could never be flushed down the toilet.

Although daily bathing is not necessary for good hygiene, baths can affect toilet training and the establishment of urinary control. That is because young children often sit in bubble baths or play in plain water baths after they have used soap or shampoo. Bathing in water that has soap particles, detergents, perfumes, or any other chemicals can cause irritation of the urethra. This irritation can be very mild or may even lead to an infection. The child may react to the irritation by trying to hold back urine until her bladder is so full that she lets some out, or by going to the potty frequently in small amounts. It is better to prevent problems by avoiding bathing in anything but plain water, saving the use of soap or shampoo until just before getting out of the tub. If a child has many wetting accidents after being toilet trained, she should be seen by her healthcare provider. She may need her urine tested for infection.

Even though it is much easier for girls to get infections, boys can become irritated from bath water and have accidents as well. Little boys who are not circumcised also need to be taught to pull back their foreskin gently to clean their penis. Without this regular cleaning, a boy may develop an odor or an infection. Cleanliness in this area is important because of health problems associated with inadequate hygiene.

It is important that all of your child's urine and bowel movements be quickly disposed of so that there is not an opportunity for growth of bacteria in the waste products. In most homes, it will be most convenient to keep a diaper pail or wastebasket with a plastic liner near any location where a child is using a potty chair. Anything that touches the urine or bowel movement that cannot be flushed away should either be washed in soap and hot water or discarded after being wrapped in plastic. Even if you are trying to minimize the use of plastic in your household, this step is necessary to protect the health of sanitation workers who pick up garbage in your community.

Parents do not have to be compulsively clean to keep their children healthy. Regular handwashing is more important for family and community health than any other activity. Teaching a child to clean up after herself promotes independence as well as good health habits.

PART THREE

COMMON TOILET
TRAINING PROBLEMS

12
HALF TRAINED

Max was able to use the potty or the toilet at home and at preschool with hardly any help. Anywhere else, it seemed like he was always wet, even with reminders. We finally decided that he could only wear underwear when he was at a place where it was easy for him to be independent. It was almost a year before he was out of diapers all day, but at least we weren't getting frustrated.

"**I**s your child toilet trained yet?" may seem like a question that can be answered "yes" or "no." However, the answer will depend in part on how you define the phrase "toilet trained." To some parents, a child is toilet trained when he can wear underpants and stay dry and accident-free throughout the day if he gets help and supervision from an adult. He is cooperative, but still needs reminders and encouragement from his parents and some assistance with clothing or cleaning up. To other parents, a child is toilet trained when he is able to independently remember to use the toilet, rarely needs prompting, and can take care of himself in the bathroom without assistance. One way to describe the child who still needs help is to call him "half trained."

There are some things that parents can do to help their child move from being half trained to using the toilet independently. During the first stage of toilet training most parents dress their children in elastic waist pants or other types of easy-to-remove clothing. As children get older, however, parents often dress them in cute outfits that may require more time or assistance to remove. If a child needs to struggle with buttons, zippers, tights, or overalls before or after going to the bathroom, the effort may discourage her from taking a break from play. If she waits until she has no choice, she may wind up having an accident.

When parents notice wet pants in a child who is often able to stay dry, the degree of wetness will offer a clue to what may be the problem. If a child is soaked or if she has a complete bowel movement in her pants, it is likely that she was not motivated enough to stop her activity to go to the bathroom. However, if the pants are simply damp or the bowel movement is very small, it is likely that the child does notice the feeling, but is trying very hard to hold on. The smaller accident is from letting go slightly to relieve pressure.

Another common pattern among half-trained children is that they are able to get to the bathroom easily at home or in familiar places, but frequently soak or soil their underpants when they are away from home. This pattern occurs when a child is mature enough to master the physical control necessary to use the toilet and stay dry, but is not old enough to be psychologically in control as well. When she is in a familiar place, she can take herself to the bathroom, perhaps with a reminder or perhaps without any help at all. Away from home, the young child has accidents because she has many new experiences to distract her and she is not paying attention to the signals from her body that say, "Time to go."

If you notice that your child has accidents when she is out but not at home, you can tell her that until she is older you want her to wear diapers when you are out. Tell her that even if she is in diapers, she can still use the bathroom if she wants to. When you go to unfamiliar places, find the bathroom when you arrive. Offer her a chance to use it then and after an hour or two. If she has not used the bathroom before it is time to leave, you can suggest that she try then. After you have practiced the away-from-home routine for several months, you will have a new routine that she can follow when you are out together. If your child is visiting somewhere without you, make sure that before you leave someone has shown her where the bathroom is and that she feels comfortable using it. Don't assume that grandparents or parents of other children will remind her or help her unless you ask them to do so. Most people simply do not think about a young child's bathroom needs unless the child is their own.

When your child forgets to go to the bathroom, whether she is at home or away from home, it is unlike to be because of carelessness. Although she may want to use the potty, she is also busy learning and doing many other things that are very important to her. She will need time to get from being half trained to being fully trained, but with patience she will get there.

13

"ONLY IN MY DIAPER"

Aaron is almost four. He took his time getting toilet trained, but he has been completely accident-free ever since he was three years old. The only problem is that he insists on a diaper for making his bowel movement. He'll even go to get one and bring it to us. We tried telling him he couldn't have one, but he just started waiting until he was in his diaper at bedtime. It doesn't seem any easier to have to go in and change him a half hour after we've said goodnight.

Some children learn to use the potty or toilet for urinating without a struggle, but resist having a bowel movement anywhere but in diapers. There are a number of variations of this pattern. Sometimes a child will happily wear underpants until he feels the sensation of needing to have a bowel movement. He will then request or demand a diaper, or if he's old enough, go to get the diaper himself. Other children don't announce a preference, but wait until a diaper is in place for a nap or at bedtime before having their bowel movement. Sometimes a child is wearing underpants part of the time, but once he's ready to have a bowel movement, he makes sure that he's wearing a diaper, and then runs to another room where he crouches or hides while he pushes out a bowel movement. Sometimes little boys are standing to urinate and get out of the habit of sitting on the toilet.

All of these types of behavior are quite natural and understandable from a young child's point of view. Even though parents see the act of passing urine and passing a bowel movement as being in the same category, a child may not feel ready to take both steps at the same time. Parents of a child trained for urination will usually begin to urge, coax, or put pressure on the child to take the next step, but the child begins to resist. The energy that he might have used to ready himself for the next step forward gets used up in his insistence that he wants to decide for himself when to take that step.

Sometimes parents are able to suggest to a child who only want to put his bowel movement in a diaper, "We know you can use the potty for your bowel movement. It's time to put the diapers away." If the child is almost ready to take the next step toward independence anyway, this approach may work.

However, if a child feels that he is being pushed along too quickly, he is likely to refuse to go along with the parents' plans. Instead of going on the potty, he just holds on to his bowel movements, holding them in instead of pushing them out. After a day or two he may let go, but instead of complying with his parents' wishes, he lets go into his pants. The mess is very unpleasant to clean up, of course, and parents may get upset and angry. If a child still doesn't want to give in, he may then keep going in his pants, knowing that it will upset his parents. Alternatively, he may hold on even longer, keeping his bowel movement inside as long as he can. If the holding-on pattern continues, he may develop the pattern of withholding and retention described in another key.

A child who insists on having a bowel movement in a diaper probably has enough control to wait for the time and place when he will let go. He is "trained," in the sense of being able to control his bowels, but he is unwilling to use the "parent-approved" site for having his bowel movement. He needs to be helped to take the next step in a way that does not foster even more resistance to using the potty or toilet.

There is no single solution to overcoming this resistance once it occurs. As with any kind of refusal around toilet training, if your child is unwilling, it is unlikely that increasing pressure will get him to change his mind. Instead, tell your child that if he wants to continue to use the diaper for now, that will be okay with you. Stop urging your child in *any* way to change his toileting habits for at least a month. That means no discussions at all!

At the same time that you are easing up on pressure about giving up the diaper, it is a good idea to make sure that your child is in other ways expected to act his age. The key on supporting competence describes the ways in which parents can help young children to feel generally self-confident about taking care of themselves. The feeling of competence that goes along with letting go of babylike behaviors and becoming more "grown-up" often will help a child to feel that he is ready to give up his diaper.

After the month has passed, tell your child that it is time to begin having "relaxed sitting time." That means having your child sit on the potty or toilet with feet on a stool while you read or talk to him. This helps your child get used to sitting without the pressure to produce. After a week of practice, have your child sit right after he has his bowel movement in his diaper. Although this may seem backward, this will help him make the connection between sitting and producing a bowel movement. After a few more weeks, if your child has a predictable time for a bowel movement, you can suggest that he sit before that time.

Many children will have a bowel movement on the potty during this time and then be able to take the next steps without any further difficulty. Some others will not. If you have continued to have relaxed sitting time for over a month and your child is still happily going in a diaper at another time of day, you'll have to decide whether to wait it out or force the issue. There is no right answer because every child's way of learning new skills is different. Most parents will have a sense of whether a child needs to be pushed or left alone based on how they have accomplished other developmental steps.

If you decide it is time to push, you can tell your child that you have decided that it is time to use up the last of the daytime diapers. Let him know that when the diapers are gone, there will not be anymore except for naps and overnight. Of course, if your child is already waking up dry, you can discontinue all diapers.

Make sure that you run out of diapers at a time when you can have a quiet weekend at home or a few days off. It's reasonable to expect that your child will be reluctant to use the potty or toilet and you don't want to have other distractions or to have him be away from home and a familiar bathroom. For several days before the weekend, it is helpful to offer your child foods that are more likely to make his bowel movements easier to pass. If you aren't sure what these are, look at the suggestions in Key 9, "Diet."

When you get to the last diaper, tell your child that you know it will be hard for him to make this change, but that you are sure that he can do it. If he gets angry or upset, don't try to talk him out of his feelings or to persuade him that he will feel better later. All you have to do is to act patient and calm, even though you may not feel that way inside. You can suggest a warm bath, a cup of hot chocolate, or any relaxing activity that may make it easier for him to let go. If he is unwilling to go, leave him alone.

Many children, if they have had a few months to forget that the issue was a struggle, will be able to use the potty or toilet at this point. However, some children will still refuse. If your child refuses to have a bowel movement the first day, you can wait and give him time to try the second day. But if two days have passed, it's best to tell your child that it is important for him to push his bowel movement out and that you can see he just doesn't feel like he can do it in the toilet. Offer him a diaper and let him use it.

Although you will be backing down from your expectations, it is important to remember that if your child can hold on to a bowel movement for two days, he may be able to hold on much longer. You do not want him to develop the pattern of withholding his bowel movements for long periods or he may wind up with a physiological problem that is harder to solve than his resistance to using the toilet.

If you have really eased up on the pressure for several months and your child is still locked into this pattern, it is time to seek help from your healthcare provider. Someone who is outside the family is often much more effective than parents in helping a child to let go of an old behavior. The same words coming from a doctor, a nurse practitioner, or even a child's teacher can be much more persuasive than when the words are spoken by a parent!

14

RESISTANCE

Kelly was fine about using the potty and was fairly successful. Then she just started to refuse. We urged her and tried offering her little prizes and treats. We were getting pretty exasperated when her preschool teacher told us that it might work better if we told her we were going to take a vacation from reminders. We put her back in diapers most of the time, but if she wanted to wear underpants at home we let her. We didn't remind her to go or say anything about accidents. After a month or so we said, "Kelly, we think you're ready to start using the potty all the time now." She said, "Okay" and she never had a problem again.

When a child does not want to cooperate with her parents' attempts to toilet train her, she can be described as being resistant. Resistance means that the child is refusing to move in the direction that the parent wishes her to go.

When a child is beginning to sit on the potty chair a few times a day while her parents talk or read to her, her cooperation may be inconsistent. She may be willing to sit every few hours one day and the next day refuse to sit at all. If parents do not insist and simply wait for a few hours or until the next day to try again, most children will become interested again. If a child persists in her refusal, parents should take this as a good sign that she is not ready to begin the toilet training process.

Respond to this resistance by waiting to begin again after a month or two.

A child who is comfortable sitting and taking some steps in the toilet training process may still show reluctance at times. It is natural for a young child to at times be reluctant to do what her parents want her to do. When you ask your child to come in for dinner and she ignores you, it does not mean that she is not hungry or does not want to join the family. It means "Not now" or "I don't want to stop what I'm doing" and most parents find that by being calm but firm the child will reluctantly stop playing and come to the table. In the same way, a child's mild refusal to use the potty does not mean that parents should stop the training process. Instead, it usually makes sense to continue to make regular, calm but firm statements that it is time to go, or to use the technique of setting a timer so that the bell signals "time to go" rather than the parent.

A child who is genuinely resistant, however, will make it clear by her words or her actions that she is unwilling to continue to use the potty. She may refuse to go at all, even when it would be convenient after a bath or a nap. Even if she sits down on the potty you may see a look on her face that signals her determination to hold back. She may tell you that she is going to wear diapers until she is four years old or that you can take the potty chair and put it in the garage because she doesn't like it any more.

When parents run into this kind of resistance, they will probably feel very frustrated. Parents who thought their child was on the way to being toilet trained are usually eager to discontinue the expense and bother of diapers. Unfortunately, the child does not think about her parent's point of view. Like all children her age, she is only concerned with herself. It is out of this conflict that tension arises between parent and child that can have the unfortunate effect of causing the child to resist even more.

If a child has been cooperative with the toilet training process and then begins to resist, parents can try these approaches:

- Make sure that you are not expressing anger or disappointment with your child because of accidents. In order for a child to independently use the toilet, she has to feel that the achievement is for herself, not just to please a parent.
- Look at the way in which you are asking or urging your child to use the potty. Sometimes if parents decrease the number of reminders or lighten the tone of their voices, a child's resistance disappears. Even parents who believe that they are allowing their child to move at her own pace may be applying pressure in the tone of their voice that they do not notice but the child does. You can try switching to use a timer as a reminder or you can stop reminding the child at all.
- Make sure that other factors are not making it hard for your child to cooperate. A busy schedule, changes in routine, or family stresses may be taking her energy away from her interest in using the potty. Her resistance may be her way of saying that toilet training is "too much" for her right now.

There is no single solution for overcoming a child's resistance once it occurs. If you find yourself trying numerous methods to get your child to cooperate and she continues to refuse or resist, it is a good idea to take a break. Tell your child that it is time to take a vacation from practicing or from trying to stay dry all day. If your child is in underwear, it may be a good idea to return to diaper use again, as long as you don't present the change as a punishment.

In a large study at the University of Pennsylvania School of Medicine, researchers found that when a group of children who were partially trained but resistant to using the potty or toilet for bowel movements were returned to wearing diapers in a nonpunitive manner, 90 percent of them became fully toilet trained within three months. Although no one can say for sure how long one should interrupt the toilet training process when a child is resistant, a month is probably the minimum break.

After waiting at least a month, you can introduce toilet training practice again. Most children will be willing to try again at this point and will be much more successful. If your child is still unwilling, or if she is acting angry or upset about the issue, talk to your healthcare provider. It is often helpful to get an outside point of view and many children respond very well to the interest and attention of someone outside the family who can help them get back on track.

15

REGRESSION

When Ellen was two she was almost trained to use the potty when the holidays rolled around. At first she was delighted to show her grandparents how well she was doing. Then all the cousins were around showing off their achievements, and I don't think she felt as special. After the first week of house guests, she started wetting her new underwear and making puddles around the house. We realized that she just wasn't ready to stay dry when there were so many other things going on. So we took a break until January and then she got back on track.

We didn't realize Peter was aware that we were having problems in our marriage until he started having accidents at preschool and on weekends. He'd been having trouble going to bed at night, too. At first we thought he was just acting up, but then we realized he was upset. Once we started to keep our disagreements in front of him to a minimum, the accidents almost disappeared and he started sleeping better.

Leah was using the toilet at home and a potty at her first preschool. When she changed schools and she had trouble going to the bathroom, the teachers thought she wasn't used to a regular toilet. She even told one of the teachers that she wore diapers at home, even though she was almost four years old! We figured out that she was just reacting to all the changes in school, my work hours, and meeting new teachers. We gave her time, and she started being able to use the bathroom at school as well as she did at home.

Children are continually developing new skills and behaviors that are associated with growing up. Once children have learned to dress themselves, to feed themselves, or to use the toilet independently we usually expect them to be able to continue to do these things. Sometimes, however, a child will seem to lose his ability to be competent in one or more areas that he has previously mastered. This loss of abilities is called regression. Regression means taking a step backward. A child begins to act the way he did when he was younger.

The step backward is most often the loss of the skill a child has recently acquired. The child who has been dressing himself will suddenly be unable to do so without help. The child who has been falling asleep easily at night will want an extra story or a drink of water or to have someone lie down with him. A child who has been able to get himself to the toilet or potty without being reminded starts to have many accidents every day.

Often the child's regression occurs at a time when he or the family is having to adapt to a change. Sometimes the change is one that is easy to recognize as being stressful, such as the birth of a sibling or parents arguing. Positive changes and transitions such as holidays or vacations also can be stressful. Even when parents understand that a child is reacting to stress, they may be very unhappy if the child they thought had learned how to get to the toilet seems to be having many accidents. If parents are already dealing with changes, the extra work of a child's accidents may be even more upsetting.

Parents are usually more patient with children and there- fore better able to respond effectively when they understand how the regressive behavior actually helps a child to cope with stress. It also helps to recognize that regression is common in children and adults. Most people, at times of stress, turn to familiar childlike pleasures for comfort. An adult who is upset might want a glass of warm milk, a favorite food, or a bubble bath. She might wish she could crawl into bed and pull the covers up over her head! If an adult can feel this way, it is not surprising that a child under stress would want to behave in a way that is more babylike. Even if your child is only three years old, he has to go backward in time to feel the comfort of acting younger.

When a child regresses in an area in which he used to be independent, he may receive another benefit. The more inde- pendent he is, the less attention he may get from the adults around him. When he is feeling very secure inside, he enjoys the feelings of competence that accompany acting indepen- dently. But if he is feeling sad, lonely, or left out, he may do things that force adults to take care of him more. Even if he gets negative attention for having toileting accidents, that can be better than no attention at all.

The best way for parents to respond to any kind of regres- sion from their child is to be accepting of his desire to act younger but at the same time continue to expect him to act his age. For example, you can say to a child who has had an acci- dent, "Oh, I guess you forgot that you're not wearing diapers anymore. When you were little you could go in your diaper whenever you needed to go, but now you have to remember to get to the bathroom." If the accidents persist, act matter of fact and refrain from getting angry at your child. You can say to your child, "It's not very pleasant for either of us to have to clean up puddles or wash out pants. We can remind you to go more often and that will help." Telling a child that he is acting like a baby or scolding him rarely is helpful and may increase the regressive behavior.

If accidents are constant or if adults can't refrain from scolding or being angry, it may be better to return to diapers for a few weeks, telling your child that you're going to take a "vacation" from underpants for a little while. However, if he has been in underpants for months and the accidents are not frequent, it is better to continue to consider him "trained" and to not switch back. Try to avoid getting angry and avoid getting into punitive responses such as forcing a child to do his laundry. Instead, tell your child that since he has learned to stay dry most of the time, you're sure that he will soon be able to stay dry all of the time. Be relaxed and matter of fact and ask him to help you mop up puddles, in the same way as you react if he spills a glass of milk.

Many times the stress that seems to be the cause of the child's regression can be alleviated once parents know that it is a problem. Other times they cannot change whatever circumstances the family or the child is experiencing. Even if you cannot change the circumstances that have caused the stress, you can almost always help your child to cope better if you slow down the pace of his daily activities as much as possible and spend a little quiet time with him every day.

PART FOUR

MORE CHALLENGING PROBLEMS

16
CONSTIPATION

Aaron has always been irregular. Sometimes he'll have two bowel movements a day, sometimes only one, sometimes none at all. We called the doctor because we thought he was constipated. But the doctor told us that if his bowel movements were always soft and seemed easy for him to push out we shouldn't worry.

Danny was so excited about having bowel movements in his new potty that he hardly ever had an accident. Then we went on vacation and his routine changed. Sometimes he didn't go for a day or two. One day he pushed out a big hard rock and he cried. I knew he had hurt himself because there was a little blood when we wiped him. It seems like after that, his bowel movements only happen every few days and sometimes they are very hard.

Sometimes Maria tries to have a bowel movement and she just can't. Her face gets all red and she bends over, but she doesn't push anything out. When she finally goes, first there are lots of small hard pieces and then a big piece that looks pretty soft.

The doctor told Aaron's parents that Aaron's bowel movements were normal. Aaron wasn't having difficulty with elimination and his bowel movements were always soft.

Aaron just had an irregular and unpredictable pattern. His parents didn't need to worry.

Parents used to be urged to make sure that their children had daily bowel movements. They were told that a lack of "regularity" was a problem for the child's overall health. If a child didn't produce a daily bowel movement, he might be given a dose of a "remedy," a laxative, or even an enema to cleanse him out. The pursuit of "regularity" probably contributed to many children developing problems with bowel movements rather than curing them.

Danny and Maria, however, are producing bowel movements that are often dry and hard. Both children seem to be uncomfortable when they are trying to eliminate. Danny's hard bowel movement probably broke the skin around his anus causing what is called an *anal fissure,* a small shallow tear that is very painful and can take time to heal because of its location. This painful experience may make him avoid trying to go to the potty because he doesn't want to feel hurt again. Maria's parents say that because of her red face and crouched position it looks as if she is trying to "go," but she also may be clenching her muscles to avoid going if her bowel movement feels hard and uncomfortable to her when it comes out. Both children are constipated.

A constipated bowel movement is one that is hard and dry. The larger it is, the more likely it is that the child will resist letting it pass. Unfortunately, it is almost impossible to convince a young child that it is a good idea to push out a bowel movement that he thinks will hurt him. The sooner that parents recognize constipation and begin to treat it, the less likely it is that a child will develop patterns of withholding bowel movements that can lead to long-term difficulties.

The first step that parents should take if they notice a hard or dry bowel movement is to look at a child's diet and make the changes suggested in Key 9 "Diet." If your child does not drink very much, try to increase the amount of fluid she takes in every day, preferably by encouraging more water. If your child is willing, adding two to four ounces of prune juice or four to six dried prunes to the child's daily diet can be very effective. Some children will also respond well to pear nectar. If your child eats many fatty or greasy foods, cut back on them, because these foods tend to fill children up and prevent them from being hungry for other foods that may have more fiber in them. However, some fat is important for elimination, so if your child tends to eat a very low-fat diet, she may need some extra oil or butter added to her food.

In addition to changing your child's diet, notice if there is a time during the day when your child is most likely to have a bowel movement. If there is, make sure that time is as relaxed as possible. In general, try to slow down your pace so that there is time after meals for your child to relax. A two or three year old who is rushing around may not be relaxing enough to have a bowel movement. If you've noticed your child straining or if you've seen cracked skin around her anus, you can apply a small dab of petroleum jelly at the opening several times a day to keep her comfortable and to prevent or aid healing an anal fissure.

If changing your child's diet doesn't work within a week, or if your child resists eating high-fiber foods, it is important to consult your child's healthcare provider. Your child may need an oral stool softener or a laxative at this point. This type of medication should only be prescribed by someone familiar with managing children's constipation. The initial dose and the subsequent doses need to be monitored closely. Some children will need short-term help, others will need longer-term help, but these decisions should be made with professional advice. Medication is often an excellent solution to help a young child regain good bowel patterns, but parents will need help deciding how much to give and how long to continue.

Parents should never use suppositories or enemas without the advice of a healthcare provider. It is especially important to avoid saying to the child, "If you don't go to the toilet you'll have to have an enema!" because the child may then view the treatment as a punishment. Suppositories or enemas that are used in this way may upset a child so much that she will try even harder to hold back her bowel movement. Talking to your child's healthcare provider can help you and your child to deal with the constipation in a way that will bring relief to everyone involved.

17

WITHHOLDING BOWEL MOVEMENTS

We didn't realize that Jane had a problem at first. She was potty trained for urine at two and a half. After a while, she seemed comfortable putting her bowel movements in the potty too. At some point after she started using the big toilet we realized that she was having huge bowel movements. Then we realized that she was only going every few days. It wasn't until she skipped five days that we called the doctor, who told us that Jane must be withholding her bowel movements and that we had to help her.

The worst thing about John's withholding was that we didn't understand what was going on. He never had hard bowel movements so we didn't think he had a problem. But by the time he had gone two or three days without a bowel movement, he was clearly uncomfortable. We'd try to get him to have a bowel movement, but he'd tell us he didn't have to go, even though we could tell he was all filled up.

My sister was visiting and she saw what Melissa left in the toilet. She said, "If it takes more than one flush, there's something wrong!" She was right.

In Key 16, "Constipation," the pattern of constipation was described. Hard, dry, difficult-to-pass bowel movements are uncomfortable for a child to expel so parents usually recognize fairly quickly that there is a problem. Some children, however, develop another pattern of having bowel movements that may not be noticed for months. This is the pattern of withholding or retaining bowel movements.

In order for a child to hold on to his bowel movements, he has to ignore the feeling of pressure in his lower intestine that signals "time to go." Everyone does this occasionally, because there are times when a bathroom is not close by and it is necessary to wait. However, if a child develops a pattern of holding on to or retaining his bowel movements, a problem will develop. The wall of the intestine will gradually stretch to accommodate the larger amount of bowel movement that accumulates as he holds on after the first day. As the mass gets larger, it may become more difficult to pass. The child is more reluctant to push it out, and a cycle of withholding and retaining begins. Once a child has been retaining his bowel movements for a few months, he will become less sensitive to the "time-to-go" feeling because the muscle wall will stretch and the nerves will be less able to respond to pressure. That is why a child will tell his parents that he "doesn't have to go" because he cannot feel the sensation anymore. Sometimes parents will notice that their child is crouching forward, red faced, looking as though he is straining to push out a bowel movement. Often, that posture is seen because the child is struggling to hold a bowel movement in and he is bending over to help him clench his muscles.

Occasionally a small amount of bowel movement will pass even though the child is trying to hold it back. If the child is out of diapers, parents may notice a soiling of underwear. The soiling usually distresses everyone. The child may not even feel the small amount of bowel movement passing out. These soiling accidents can add another layer of difficulty to the problem, since the child may be scolded for not making it to the potty in time, causing him to feel shame or embarrassment for disappointing his parents and himself.

Parents who suspect that their child is withholding or retaining bowel movements should call their healthcare provider for an appointment. It is usually helpful if parents bring in a record of how often the child is having bowel movements. Include the size (small, medium, large, huge) and consistency (mushy, soft, formed, hard) of each movement. Parents may feel strange keeping this record, since they are not in the habit of looking at bowel movements closely, but it will be very valuable in helping the child's healthcare provider determine the extent of the problem.

Treatment of withholding and retention will include several steps:

- Explaining to the parents and the child that this problem is very common. Parents should not blame themselves for not recognizing it earlier or for expressing frustration to the child before they realized that the child could not control the problem on her own. In fact, if a parent of a two, three, or four year old recognizes the pattern at this age, in all likelihood they are acting early and preventing future problems. Even if the onset of the problem was associated with an episode of illness, constipation, or family stress, finding the cause is much less important than treating the difficulty.
- A review of the child's patterns of passing bowel movements in order to create the best conditions for establishing regularity. Take a break from any toilet training. If a child is already using the potty or the toilet, it will be easier to develop new elimination habits if parents provide regular times to sit and relax in order to have a bowel movement. Some children can be taught to grunt or blow on a straw or balloon to help them get the feeling of pushing.

- The child's feet should rest on a stool so that he can bear down more easily.
- Increasing fiber in the child's diet will help to make bowel movements softer and easier to pass, as described in Key 9.
- Taking advantage of the body's natural reflexes that stimulate bowel movements. Many children will be able to have a bowel movement more readily after drinking a warm beverage. The feeling of warmth and fullness at the base of the stomach usually stimulates a bowel movement after 15 minutes. Other children may be helped by taking a warm bath or by placing a warm, not hot, heating pad on their abdomen for 10 to 15 minutes.
- Daily doses of a stool softener or laxative. Many children will need to take medication for an extended period of time. Medication should be given as recommended and not decreased or stopped without medical advice. It is usually necessary to continue medication beyond the time that a child returns to having daily bowel movements. If parents discontinue medication too soon, the problem tends to recur.

Although this key describes the pattern of withholding and retention as it is seen in preschool-age children, the condition can occur in older children as well. One of the most common times for children to begin withholding is in the early years of elementary school. As children get busier, they may not have the time to relax at home to have a bowel movement. Once they are at school, the bathrooms may be less inviting or private, or they may not want to leave class or recess to take the time to go. Like younger children, they hold on as long as they can. But unlike younger children whose parents are noticing their bathroom habits, older children may continue with a withholding and retention problem for quite a long time. Usually the first sign of a problem is soiling accidents, small or large, in the child's underwear. The soiling is an overflow or leakage from the stretched-out bowel. Parents should recognize that this is a physical problem, not a behavioral problem, and schedule a medical appointment right away.

Most healthcare providers know that the problem of withholding and retention is primarily physical, not psychological. Any behavioral difficulties that have emerged as a result of tension or conflict about using the potty or toilet usually resolve quickly once the child is successfully treated medically. However, if parents feel that they are having struggles with their child about managing this issue, it is often very helpful to get additional counseling. Toileting problems are rarely a result of emotional difficulties, but they can definitely be the cause of stress for parents and children.

18

DAYTIME WETTING

Many children will have daytime wetting accidents for at least six months after they have begun using the toilet independently. For most children, the accidents occur less and less frequently as they get older, although occasional accidents would be considered normal up until age four, even if a child had been toilet trained for over a year. Sometimes parents will notice patterns of accidents that indicate a child needs to be reminded to go more often at home or at school or that a child needs extra help in using the toilet when she is in unfamiliar places. However, some children seem to have frequent wetting accidents long after they have become toilet trained and long after most children their age are accident-free. Parents may notice that reminders do not help and often cause tension.

If parents notice increased frequency of urination or that the child feels the need to urinate but only produces small amounts, an appointment should be made with the child's healthcare provider. Urinary tract infections are a common cause of daytime problems and must be evaluated and treated. If there is no evidence of infection, other causes can be explored. One common cause of daytime accidents can be irritation or mild inflammation of the urethra (the small tube that connects the bladder to the outside) caused by using a bubble bath or simply by sitting in a bathtub with soapy water or shampoo in it. Switching to plain water baths or showers can make a difference.

Sometimes a child's frequent wetting accidents are an indication that she has not taken responsibility for getting herself to the toilet. She may have learned to rely on other people to remind her to go. Or, she may resist a parent reminding her because she does not want to be told what to do. If the child is usually able to stay dry when she is away from home but has many accidents at home when her parents are there, then the resistance is to parental involvement. In order for a child to be helped with this problem, parents will have to tell her, "We know that you don't want to have accidents, but we also think that you can be in charge. If you have an accident, we'll help you clean up." Parents then have to stop reminding and allow the child to make enough mistakes to learn that her parents really are leaving it up to her.

This approach will usually work after a few weeks if a child is capable of staying dry on her own. It will not work if the child has developed a behavioral pattern of urinating that interferes with her ability to stay dry. Some children who wet during the day are holding on to their urine for as long as they can. They may get up in the morning and get involved in play or watching television and have an accident because they ignored the full sensation from their bladder until it was too late. By the time they feel the need to "go" it is too late. Sometimes the child will let go of a large amount of urine, but more often she will release a small amount, sometimes on her way to the bathroom. Parents may notice squirming behavior that they describe as the child needing to urinate, but the child is actually squirming to avoid letting urine out. Typically, the child has damp underwear much of the time, even though she goes to the toilet. These children sometimes go to the bathroom very infrequently compared to other children, claiming "I don't have to go" when asked. Sometimes, if the parent says, "It's time to go to the bathroom," rather than asking if the child wants or needs to go, the child will be able to get to the bathroom in time.

A similar pattern occurs when a child goes to the bathroom to urinate but sits down briefly. She may release some urine but she is in fact holding in more. Since the child does not completely empty her bladder, she may fill up again soon, creating the need to urinate again. She has accidents because she sometimes doesn't want to bother to get up from play, or because she has learned to tune out the sensations from her bladder.

Both of these patterns can be helped by getting a child into a routine of going to the bathroom more often and emptying completely when she goes. It is usually easier to get a child to change her habits if parents first offer her large quantities of any liquid she likes. The more that she drinks, the more urine she will produce, and the harder it will be for her to ignore the signals that it is time to go. Next, the parents will have to structure a routine for the child of going into the bathroom to try to go at least every two hours. When she urinates, she should be encouraged to try to push out more when she thinks she is finished and praised if she is able to do so. Another exercise that some children will find both helpful and fun is to stop the flow of urine by squeezing tight, then releasing to start it again. Usually a few weeks of this retraining will begin to reduce the number of accidents. The child's increased physical awareness combined with her satisfaction at being able to stay dry will help to change the underlying habits.

An often-overlooked problem that can lead to daytime wetting accidents is constipation. If a child is having hard bowel movements or has developed a new pattern of infrequent and irregular bowel movements, pressure from the bowel area may even be pushing on the bladder to decrease its capacity. Before the daytime wetting can be resolved, the child's constipation must be cured.

Most children who have been toilet trained for a year or more will have few wetting accidents during the day. It is unlikely that a child who is having accidents is doing so out of carelessness or as deliberate misbehavior. If parents observe the child's patterns they often are able to develop an approach that will work to help the child stay dry. If none of these approaches work, however, your healthcare provider should be seen again for a more comprehensive evaluation.

19

NIGHTTIME WETTING

Jeremy wets the bed at night, even when he uses the toilet right before going to sleep. He's four now and he's been toilet trained since he was two. It's frustrating for us because we'd like to be done with diapers for at least one child. Jeremy doesn't seem as upset as we are, but he can tell that we're disappointed.

Parents often feel frustrated if their child can stay dry while his is awake during the day but cannot stay dry when he is asleep. Jeremy's parents thought that his pattern was unusual. They didn't realize that night wetting is very common among young children and at Jeremy's age is considered normal. Although some children begin to stay dry at night within a few months after achieving daytime dryness, for many children this next step may not take place for several years.

Parents are usually surprised to hear that about 25 percent of all four year olds and 15 percent of five year olds wet their beds at least once a week. Most children find it easier to stay dry through the night as they grow older, but 15 percent of all six year olds still wet their beds occasionally. Nighttime wetting is more common in boys than in girls but not at all unusual in girls.

Staying dry during the night is related more to development than it is to motivation. Children who take longer than others to stay dry at night have two characteristics in common. First, they produce more urine during the night than their bladders (the place where urine collects) can comfortably hold. That may be because their bodies make a large amount of urine or because their bladders are smaller and stretch less than average. Second, once their bladders are full, the sensation of fullness does not cause them to wake up to go to the bathroom. That may be because they are less sensitive to the feeling of a stretched bladder or because they are sleeping so deeply that they don't notice when their bladder is full. Many children sleep deeply, but they all do not wet their beds. No one knows for sure why some children can awaken to go to the bathroom when their bladders are full and others continue to sleep. What we do know is that nighttime wetting is not a sign of laziness.

Nighttime wetting (which is also called *nocturnal enuresis* when a child is over five years old) often runs in families. Many times a parent, an aunt, or an uncle has had the same difficulty as the child staying dry at night. Parents sometimes remember being scolded or punished for wetting the bed when they were young. They may have felt ashamed about wetting and no one may have told their parents that the wetting was common in young children. If parents have unpleasant memories of their own difficulties staying dry at night, they may worry if their own child seems to be having similar difficulties. It is usually helpful to talk to your child's healthcare provider about any worries you have about this issue.

Parents have an important role in helping their child solve the problem of wetting the bed. Even if you have made the mistake of becoming angry with your child about a wet bed, it is never too late to tell him that you now know that the wetting isn't his fault. Parents can also express confidence that their child will learn to stay dry all night in the same way he has learned to do other things on his own. They can point out that there are some things that he has learned quickly, maybe faster than his friends, and that some kids learn other things faster than he does. They can remind him that he has already figured out how to stay dry during the day. A parent can say, "You know how during the day, when you notice you 'have to go' you decide whether to go to the bathroom right away or hold your pee inside you for a while? Well, the next thing you are going to learn is how to do that during the night. You haven't learned yet to do the same thing while you are sleeping, but you will learn it, for sure." This kind of positive attitude from parents will create an expectation for a child that is very powerful.

Once a child who is wearing diapers at night is able to stay dry for more than a week, either by holding his urine or by waking himself to go to the bathroom, it is reasonable to allow him to try sleeping without diapers. However, it is also a good idea to keep expectations realistic. A four year old may have a few weeks of dry nights and then begin to have frequent accidents. If you showered your child with praise for staying dry at night and he has a relapse, you do not want him to feel as though he has failed. If accidents persist, you may want to return to diapers and try again after a few weeks or months.

If a child has been dry at night for several months and then begins to wet the bed, he should be checked by his healthcare provider to make sure that there is not an underlying infection or illness causing the return to wetting. Sometimes a step backward in nighttime dryness is a result of other stresses in the child's life. Beginning a new school, the birth of a new baby, a change in sitters, or family tension can be the cause of wetting the bed. It is important to address underlying stresses rather than to treat wetting the bed as the problem.

Following are some common approaches for keeping children dry at night and the pros and cons of each one.

- Have your child try to use the toilet at the beginning of the bedtime routine and then again right before going to sleep.

Some children do not empty completely when they go to the bathroom, and this gives them another chance.

- Take your child to use the toilet at your own bedtime or in the middle of the night. This method may prevent your child from wetting the bed or reduce soaking, but it will probably not help him learn to stay dry independently.

- Put a night-light in the child's room, and another in the bathroom. Some children do not like to leave their rooms if it is dark around them. You can also put a potty chair near the bed. Keeping the child's room warm at night may help since some children will wet more if they are chilly, and other children will not want to get out of bed if the room is cold.

- Encourage your child to drink more liquids earlier in the day. If your child does not drink very much during the day, he may be thirsty after dinner and then will be more likely to wet during the night. It is not a good idea to restrict fluids after dinner, since most children will view the restriction as a punishment. Fruit juice and sweet drinks can increase nighttime urination, so limit after-dinner liquids to water.

- Once a child is able to stay dry several nights a week, he may like to have a chart where dry nights can be marked with stars or stickers. Some children love this approach, but others get so disappointed in themselves that they get discouraged. Use this approach only if your child is enjoying it.

- Some people feel that a child will not learn to stay dry as long as he is in diapers. However, if a young child usually wets the bed at night, wearing a diaper will be less work for parents. If a child is wearing a diaper at night, a parent should take him to the bathroom when he wakes up in the morning, remove his diaper, and have him sit on the toilet. If a child does not want to wear a diaper at night, he should be expected to help remove wet sheets and to put them and any wet clothing in the washing machine. It will help if the mattress is kept covered with plastic and a towel wrapped plastic pad is placed on top of the sheets for quicker clean up. Helping should be seen as a responsibility that goes along with deciding to sleep without diapers, not as a punishment for wetting the bed.

- If the bed wetting has not resolved by the time a child is seven or eight years old, he can try using a moisture-sensitive "alarm" device. These alarms are attached to underpants or pajamas and vibrate and sound off when he first wets his clothing or bed. The noise will awaken the parents to get the child to the bathroom. Eventually, the child will be awakened by the bell and, later on, by the vibration. Over time, these devices are extremely successful for highly motivated older children and highly motivated parents. They are not as useful for younger children because children under seven often cannot sustain motivation for the weeks or months of practice needed to get to regularly dry nights.
- In the past, medications were prescribed for children who wet the bed at night. However, today this method of treatment is usually not advisable. It is best to schedule a conference with your child's healthcare provider to discuss the risks, costs, and benefits of such treatment.

Even though nighttime wetting is described as a problem, it is perfectly normal for many young children. The most important role for parents in helping a child is to let him know that even though his wetting is frustrating, many other children have the same difficulty at his age.

PART FIVE

WORKING WITH OTHERS

20

WORKING PARENTS

Parents who are away from home during the day have a lot to juggle when they return. If parents are trying to get dinner on the table, wash a load of clothes, pick up the toys on the kitchen floor, and still have the time for enjoying being a family, adding on the routine of learning to use the potty can seem like too much. In fact, the increase in families where both parents are working outside the home is probably one of the reasons why most children are becoming toilet trained later than they were thirty years ago. When parents choose to spend their limited time with their child playing games or reading books or just relaxing, they are making a good choice.

Of course, no matter how busy parents are in the morning and evening, they will eventually have to include some toilet training activities in their time with their child. The gradual method of training makes it possible for parents to begin teaching toileting skills by helping a child get used to new patterns and routines when the family is at home.

Children are usually more successful in becoming toilet trained if they can expect a predictable daily routine. A morning routine is not the same as a morning rush. It will help if you review the tasks that need to be done each morning before you leave home and in the evening when you return. Most parents find that planning a sequence of tasks and sticking to it results in less whining or arguing and that the whole family is happier and more relaxed when they are together.

Try to have a morning routine that includes some cuddling or special time, even if it is just for a few minutes. Many children like to climb into bed with their parents for a hug. During this time you can talk to your child about the day, what she is going to do, who she will play with, the weather, and any special activities. This time is important, because if you don't give your child positive attention in the morning, she's sure to demand negative attention by resisting you or arguing with you when you are trying to get her ready to leave home. Some parents find that they need to awaken earlier in the morning to make the morning routine be more relaxed.

Have a routine for taking off the nighttime diaper, getting dressed, and eating breakfast. If your child knows what to expect, it is easier for her to cooperate with each step. When you begin toilet training, an ideal time to do the first "practice sitting" is right after you remove your child's diaper. Most families find that it works much better to get a child ready to go in the morning before allowing her to play or watch television. A good way to tell if your morning routine is working is to notice if your child is negotiating with you. If she is, it's because she thinks that the morning is flexible and that she has choices. It's hard to get to work on time if you are too flexible in the morning.

At the end of your work day, you will begin what has been called the second shift of working parents. Your next shift probably begins with picking up your child from child care or greeting her as you walk in the door at home. This reunion time is very important for both the child and the parent and it is the time that sets the stage for the rest of the evening. To help unwind from your day, take just 15 minutes to settle in with your child. After you do that, she will feel cared for and you will feel less guilty as you do all of the tasks that you need to do to get started on the evening routine. If you make your next step going to change out of your work clothes, you can bring your child along and have her try sitting again on the potty chair. Reading the mail, checking the phone messages, and making dinner can all come later.

Your evening routine will probably include dinner, playtime, bath, and bedtime. Since many young children will eat better if dinner is served early, some parents offer a child a nutritious snack to eat while dinner is being prepared. The snack, especially it if it warm, may stimulate your child to need to "go," so the routine may help in the toilet training process. If your child has not sat on the potty since you arrived home, the time after snack or dinner may wind up being a good time to have a practice on the potty session.

For many children, bath time is a relaxing and enjoyable event, and for these children an evening bath is a welcome routine. However, if your child doesn't like baths, there's no reason to make her take one more often than every few days. Washing her hands and face is adequate for hygiene, and you'll avoid unnecessary hassles. The nights when your child does take a bath, try having her use the potty before or after getting into the tub.

The next step is bedtime. The bedtime routine will go more smoothly if it is kept separate from other activities. It is usually better to have a short routine that you can repeat every night rather than a more elaborate series of activities that can only take place when you aren't too tired or busy. If you do have to be out in the evening, it is easier for a sitter to follow a short routine and to substitute for you. Bedtime is not a good time to practice using the potty because it makes it too easy for a child to use her sitting time as a way of prolonging the time before she goes to sleep.

On weekends you can include potty practice when you are at home. You will still probably want to have as your first priority enjoying your child, not using the toilet. However, keep in mind that for many children, spending leisurely time at home with parents on the weekend is a pleasure. If spending weekends at home using the potty results in more overall relaxed attention from parents, that may be your child's best motivation to be successful.

21

WHEN GRANDPARENTS HELP

When Jordan was born, I sometimes disagreed with my mom's advice about taking care of her, but we always worked things out. Now that Jordan spends many whole days with her, some of our differences are a little harder to deal with, especially when my mom tells me she can take care of getting Jordan toilet trained. But how do you disagree with someone who's raised three kids and has five grandchildren already?

It can be a blessing when grandparents are available to help care for a grandchild, but it's not unusual for parents and grandparents to disagree at times. Most often the involvement of the grandparent is so appreciated by the parents and so welcomed by the child that any differences in child-rearing philosophies can be overcome. Some differences are talked out, but many can just be ignored. However, even though a young child can easily adjust to different rules with grandparents about eating cookies or bedtime or putting feet on the sofa, it can be confusing if grandparents have different expectations than parents about toilet training.

Grandparents often want to start toilet training sooner than parents. The child-rearing practices of a generation ago were not as concerned with being "child-centered" as they are today. "Child-centered" refers to a way of guiding children that tries to allow children to show readiness or interest before parents begin real teaching or training. However, many grandparents believe that waiting for a child to decide what he is ready or interested in doing is not providing enough structure.

Other grandparents may have the desire to be indulgent toward their grandchildren, even if that was not their style in raising their own children. They may tell parents who are initiating toilet training or other activities to slow down and not push so hard. They may be feeling protective toward a grandchild, but their protectiveness may sound like criticism to their own children. Sometimes grandparents have unspoken general criticism about the way their grandchildren are being cared for that they try to keep to themselves, but the criticism comes out in comments about toilet training. A grandparent may compare a grandchild to another in a way that implies criticism of the child or the parents. All of these patterns can affect attitudes toward toilet training.

It is unlikely that differences in philosophy and approach about how or when to be toilet trained will make a difference to a young child. If grandparents are caring for your child several days a week or more you can discuss what they would like to try and the reasons why. Even if a two year old doesn't seem "ready" to Mom and Dad, he might be ready enough to practice using the potty part-time with Grandma. Since a toddler usually will not have the same kind of need to assert independence or act negatively toward grandparents as he does toward his own parents, he may be able to be more cooperative in learning when he is with them.

If grandparents do not want to participate in toilet training even if the parents have begun, a child can adapt to the expectations of each. It is not reasonable to ask a grandparent to add toilet training activities to the time spent with a grandchild if the grandparent does not feel comfortable doing so. The child will sense the discomfort and probably not do as well anyway. It's possible that changing expectations in each setting will cause the toilet training process to last longer, but if a child is ready to be trained he will still move ahead. Grandparents may be much more willing to participate once a child is having few accidents.

If grandparents are more eager to begin toilet training than you are and you decide to let them begin the training process, the best way to judge whether there is a problem is by watching your child. If he is enjoying being with his grandparents and is cooperative with the toilet training when he is with them, there is no reason to be concerned. However, if he starts to express negative feelings about diapers, using the potty, or being cared for by his grandparents, you will have to intervene. If you emphasize that the most important reason for your child to be with his grandparents is for them to have a good relationship, not to become toilet trained, you are likely to be able to get them to slow down.

Above all, grandparents, just like parents, should avoid viewing the child's success as such an achievement that if a child has an accident he feels that he has let them down. Grandparents, like parents, should keep from scolding or punishing a child for toileting mistakes. Perhaps most important, your child should never be caught in the middle of any disagreement among adults about toilet training.

22

CHILD CARE

When your child is cared for by other adults during the day, you will have to share many decisions with them. Ideally, parents should choose child-care settings where they are comfortable with the caregiver's philosophy and style of caring for children. However, you may have chosen a child-care provider long before your child was ready for toilet training, when the subject seemed too far in the future to discuss. Or you may be planning a change in care during the time that your child will probably be learning to use the potty. It is also possible that you will find a child-care setting that you like very much, but the caregiver's expectations for toilet training are different than your child's current capabilities. Even though these toilet training issues are usually just a small part of your child's overall day and experience in child care, they can become significant issues if you and the caregivers are not in agreement.

If you are looking for child care, asking questions about toilet training philosophy is a useful way of finding out how flexible the caregivers will be on that issue, but may also give you insight into the general approach you can expect with other issues. If a caregiver expects all toddlers to be ready to use the potty by a certain age, that may indicate a general lack of flexibility. A caregiver who expects children to be different from one another in their readiness for toilet training is probably going to be more flexible in other areas as well.

Good communication between parents and caregivers is important. Some brief check in should take place at the beginning and end of every day, even if everyone is in a rush. If parents do not regularly spend time in the morning or evening informally talking with the caregivers, it is important to arrange time for conferences. Parents need to know how a child is doing in child care, and caregivers need to know how a child is doing at home. With this kind of ongoing communication, it will be much easier to plan beginning toilet training.

Caregivers sometimes see a child as more ready to begin toilet training than parents do. In part, this is because children usually act more mature and capable when they are away from their parents. The difference in the way the child behaves with caregivers is not necessarily because the parents have lower expectations or child-rearing skills. It is because when children are with their parents they can relax and act younger and more dependent. They also usually need to act out many of the negative feelings they have had to control while they were with other children and adults all day.

It is useful to observe your child in child care and to find out from the teachers what she can do for herself when she is there. If your child is capable of doing things away from home that you had not thought she could, you may be underestimating her abilities. However, you may find that she is willing to do some things for this caregiver that she does not want to do for you simply because she is not ready to be that capable all day and evening.

You may want to show your caregiver the signs of readiness for toilet training described in this book. In that way, you will be making a decision together about timing. If the ideas presented are new to her, you will also be able to provide this information to her early in the process. If both you and the caregiver agree that your child is not showing signs of readiness to begin toilet training, you will both be comfortable waiting.

If you think your child is ready to begin, consulting with your caregiver first will be a good way to make her an ally. You can discuss what you would like to do at home and what can be done at child care. Keep in mind that any plan, including the one described in this book, should be viewed as a guide, not as inflexible directions. If you and your caregiver plan together, you may find that her knowledge about your child will help you in making plans for your approach at home.

Occasionally parents will be told by a child's caregivers that they have begun toilet training the child already. It is usually very upsetting for parents to be told that this decision has been made without discussion with them. Even if the child's caregivers feel that the child is ready and willing to participate in toileting activities in child care, the caregivers need to seek the parents' involvement. Without discussion, caregivers would not know if other factors need to be considered. Perhaps the family is ready to go on vacation, or Mom is pregnant, or Grandma is sick and Mom is going to be flying to another state for a week to stay with her. Caregivers need to plan toilet training in light of the whole family's needs.

If your caregiver does take this kind of step, and it is an unusual way for her to act, it may be that your child is more ready than you have realized and the caregiver is tiring of changing diapers. Talk to her and see if you can work out a compromise that works for your child. If, on the other hand, this is a familiar pattern, you may want to consider whether this lack of communication is in your child's overall best interest. The best child care takes place when caregivers and parents are acting in partnership.

If toilet training is taking place in child care and your child begins to resist, caregivers should decrease or eliminate pressure on the child. Just as parents may find that problems get worse if they try to overcome the child's resistance with pressure, caregivers are likely to have the same experience.

What is worse, however, is that a child's resistance to the toilet training pressure may spread to his not wanting to go to child care at all, which can be a very difficult problem for working parents. Since most children tend to be generally more cooperative with caregivers than they are with parents, this kind of resistance should be taken very seriously.

Sometimes parents want to enroll their child in a child-care setting that requires that children be out of diapers. Parents should ask about this policy. Sometimes the caregivers are able to care for children who are out of diapers, but need reminders and help and who still have occasional accidents. Other times, the expectation is that the child will be independently using the toilet. Even though there is no relationship between a child's other developmental and intellectual abilities and his ability to use the toilet, caregivers may be very clear about how they want to structure their program. Sometimes a program does not have the staff available to take the time with children needing help with toilet training. If caregivers are unwilling to change diapers, it is not fair to ask them to accommodate your child. It is also not a good idea to tell your child that he cannot go to a program because he is in diapers. This kind of pressure is unlikely to be effective and may well backfire because many children will refuse to become toilet trained with this kind of threat. It is not a good idea to tell child-care providers that a child is toilet trained if she is not. If your child still needs to be in diapers, you will probably have to continue to look for child care that is more flexible.

If a child is already in child care and is not being allowed to be with peers because she is not yet toilet trained and they are, parents should be concerned. If a child is being asked to spend his day with children who are younger and developmentally behind her level of play and activities because of being in diapers, she may feel as though she is being punished. If she feels angry, sad, or ashamed because of her use of diapers, she is less likely to develop the feelings of confidence she needs to be toilet trained. Holding a child back for this reason is likely to delay toilet training even longer.

If your child is having any toilet training problems, it is often helpful to discuss them with her caregiver. However, remember that even an experienced caregiver has not dealt with as many variations or problems in toilet training as a healthcare provider, so be sure to get consultation in that way as well.

23
STARTING KINDERGARTEN

Steven was using the toilet fine for over a year before he started kindergarten. We didn't even notice when or if he used the bathroom. All of a sudden he's coming home with wet pants! Sometimes he says, "I forgot," but other times he acts as if he didn't even notice!

Samantha loves to wear dresses. After she had been in first grade for a few weeks, I thought I was smelling urine on her clothes. Sure enough, her panties were damp. We talked to her and she acted as though she didn't know what we were talking about. Then I found some rolled up underwear in the back of her closet—she was hiding the accidents. We've told her that the other kids will notice the smell if she doesn't get to the bathroom, but she doesn't seem to be willing to try.

Most of the advice in this book is directed toward parents of preschool-age children who are learning to be independent in using the toilet. Once a young child is toilet trained, parents usually assume that the task is mastered and there are no further steps to take. However, the time of transition from preschool to kindergarten can be a time when children who have never had any toilet training difficulties at all may begin to have accidents.

For most children, the change from preschool to regular school represents a big leap. Even if a child has been in a large group in preschool, the threshold of the kindergarten door is a passageway to a new kind of relationship between the child and his teachers. The teacher will have higher expectations of the children in the class for behavior, cooperation, and independence.

At school, the new kindergartener is trying to learn many new things all at once. There are new rules, activities, and the challenge of beginning to learn to read. Even though the child may be very happy with his teacher, his friends, and all of the exciting things he is learning, he may still be feeling stress from the new experiences. The stress alone is enough to cause some children to have occasional accidents, but usually there are other factors involved. If a parent is aware of potential causes of accidents the child may be able to avoid having as many or any at all.

In some kindergartens, the teachers do not always include bathroom breaks as part of the day. In preschool, most children are either told that it is time to use the bathroom or they are encouraged to go at certain times, such as before snack or after nap. In regular school, even if there are many breaks during the day when a child could stop at the bathroom on the way in or out of the classroom, he may not be reminded to go. Many kindergarten classrooms have their own bathrooms. This is an advantage, since the child doesn't have to leave the room and walk down a hallway to a bathroom shared by much older kids. But the convenience of the bathroom may cause the teacher to assume that the children don't need extra help.

A group of kindergarteners, when asked why they sometimes didn't use the bathroom in their class, came up with a number of answers that were a surprise to the teacher. "Because it's dark in there until you turn on the light and I can't reach the light before the door closes." "Because it smells funny." "Because when I come out everyone knows I just went to the bathroom." "Because the window is open and the seat is really cold." "Because the sign says 'occupied' all the time." The last comment was made by a five year old who was reading very well. He didn't realize that the other children didn't change the sign because they couldn't read yet. The same boy came up with a solution to his problem: "If I have to use the bathroom, I count all of the children who are in the room. I have to remember if anyone is absent, and I have to remember to count myself. If everyone is in the room, then I know that the bathroom is really empty and I can go in."

Probably the most common reason that children have wetting accidents at school is that they don't notice the need to go to the bathroom until it's too late. Children who are very bright, persistent, and able to focus are often the most likely to have accidents because they are concentrating so hard on their work. Sometimes children are so interested in what they are learning that they are afraid to miss anything by leaving the room to go to the bathroom. Sometimes a child doesn't notice that his bladder is full until it is so full that he has to let go of a small amount of urine just to be able to get to the toilet without letting it all out. Other children may get to the bathroom, but are in such a hurry to finish that they don't empty their bladders completely and have to go again an hour later.

Teachers are usually unaware that children in the class are having difficulties staying dry. A parent might notice that a child is squirming or fidgeting in the way he usually does when he has to go, but to the teacher he might look like any other squirmy or fidgety child. A teacher might notice if a child made a large puddle on the rug, but most accidents are small. A teacher who is busy teaching is unlikely to pay attention to a damp spot on a child's trousers or skirt.

Parents who see the damp circles or patches on a child's clothing often assume that the child is "peeing in his pants." Usually the child is not letting go of any more than a dribble, just enough to feel temporarily comfortable. A small amount of liquid can appear quite large when it is placed on fabric. Try pouring a tablespoon of water on your child's pants and you will see that even a little bit of urine might be responsible for what you thought was a big accident.

Even tiny amounts of urine will begin to give off an unpleasant odor after an hour or so. The odor will of course bother parents and may be strong enough to be smelled by other children at school, although they may not recognize what it is. However, the child will probably not be aware of the odor himself. That is because after an odor is present for a while it is not noticed by someone who is smelling it all the time. That is why it is hard to smell perfume or aftershave lotion a little while after you put it on yourself, but you can smell it when someone else is wearing it. So if parents tell the child that his wetting is a problem because he smells bad, the child will not understand what the parent is talking about.

Helping Children Cope

If your child was completely toilet trained before starting kindergarten, it is reasonable to assume that he is competent in his overall ability to take care of himself at school. It is unlikely that he wants to have accidents. Often, when a child is upset about having accidents but doesn't know how to solve the problems that are causing him to have them, he may deal with his feelings of shame by pretending that he doesn't care. If he is embarrassed or fearful of being scolded or punished, he may hide the wet clothing, hoping that his accident won't be discovered.

Parents can help children cope with the problem of having accidents in kindergarten in two ways. The first is by planning ahead to avoid potential difficulties, and the second is by working with the child and the teachers at school if problems arise anyway.

It is helpful to most children who are beginning kindergarten to visit before school starts. You may not be able to meet the teacher, and sometimes the rooms are not completely set up for teaching, but you can usually walk around. Notice where all of the bathrooms are, go in, and if your child is able, have him try out the facilities.

When you meet your child's teacher, find out about rules and routines for going to the bathroom. If your child stays for an after-school program, ask which bathrooms the children use and whether the younger children are given reminders or any supervision. After your child has been in school for a few days, ask him to explain to you when the children use the bathroom and what the rules are. Ask him, "Do any of the children in your class ever have trouble getting to the bathroom in time?" Your child will have an easier time telling you about any difficulties he is having if you ask about other children rather than directing the question at him. Of course, it is very likely that what he tells you will be true for him as well.

If your child does have accidents at school or you notice damp patches on clothing once he comes home, you can first talk to him about ideas for getting to the bathroom sooner. Try not to talk to your child in a way that will make him feel embarrassed. Instead, ask him what ideas he has about how he can stay dry. Since he is probably not having accidents throughout the day, ask him, "What are the times that you get to the bathroom when you have to go? How are you able to do that?" In that way your child can focus on what he is doing right rather than on what he is doing wrong.

If talking to your child doesn't help, the next step is to talk to the teacher. Most children will not be able to talk to the teacher themselves because the subject will embarrass them. You can ask the child to join you for a discussion or you can have a conversation without him. Ask the teacher for ideas or suggestions. Most teachers will not want the responsibility of keeping track of one child, but most teachers also want to create an atmosphere where all the children can be comfortable. A teacher might be willing to give a reminder before recess to one child or the whole class. Some teachers are not aware that any children are having difficulty, but once informed they are usually very willing to help.

At home, ask you child to figure out how long he can go without needing to go to the bathroom in the evening and on the weekend. Ask him to figure out how much he can drink in order to "hold on" for two hours or three hours or four hours. Figure out with him how his ability to "hold" fits with his times for recess or lunch.

Some children respond well to small rewards for dry days. It is usually best to give small, frequent rewards rather than to have a child work toward a reward that is bigger but in the distant future. Keep in mind that the best reward to the child for staying dry should be his own sense of competence, not an external reward.

If despite your efforts your child continues to have frequent accidents or if your child begins to have accidents at home on the weekends, he should be evaluated by his health-care provider in order to rule out any medical problems that could be causing the wetting.

PART SIX

FAMILY LIFE

24

SUPPORTING COMPETENCE

We didn't realize that Patty was acting more babyish than other children her age until she started preschool. She was always so easygoing at home that it never seemed to be a problem that she needed help with everything, whether it was getting dressed or picking up toys or even feeding herself some of the time. Once we started expecting more from her, she seemed to act more grown up, and that was when she started to use the potty without being reminded to go.

art of helping your child to be independent in using the toilet is helping her to be independent in every way that she can. You have probably already learned how to help her to face different types of challenges and feel successful. For example, if she likes to do puzzles you know to choose a puzzle for her that is not so easy that she is bored, but not so difficult that she gets discouraged. If she likes to play ball, you play with the size of ball that a young child can catch with some ease and gradually teach her to move her arms and hands to catch the ball successfully. When you are teaching your child to use the toilet, you will want to make it as easy as you can for her to feel successful while she gradually learns more skills with your help.

Most parents begin toilet training by using a portable potty chair that can be placed close to where a child is playing. Doing so can make it easier for a child to stop what she is doing and get to the potty quickly. However, after the child is done using the potty, it is a good idea to go with the child to the bathroom to empty the potty and to clean up. You want your child to understand that part of being a "big kid" is to use the bathroom.

Once your child is three years old, even if she is still wearing diapers, it will help her to think of herself as being older if you stop using a changing table. Even though using a changing table is easier for parents, it is not ideal for helping a child to feel more grown up. When your child is lying on a changing table, she is in a very dependent, babylike position. Her only choices are to cooperate with your changing her or rebel against your changing her. Instead, when she needs her diapers or training pants changed, have her go with you to the bathroom. She can help to take her diaper or clothing off and put it in the wastebasket or hamper and you can then do the same wiping and washing hands that you would do if she were completely toilet trained.

A child who can undress and dress herself with ease will be much more successful in using the toilet and in feeling competent. Two and three year olds can be more independent if they are wearing pants with elastic waists that are easy to pull up or down. Other clothing choices are less important for using the toilet, but if your child is used to help getting dressed because of difficult buttons or sleeves on her clothing, it will be harder to expect her to want to dress herself. Some parents find that it is easier to help a child get dressed on weekday mornings if time is limited. They have a child practice dressing and undressing in the evenings and on weekends when it is easier for them to be patient and relaxed.

It is also helpful to encourage your child to do other things at home that are "big kid" activities. Sometimes parents are not sure what their child can do by herself. It is a good idea to notice or ask at your child's preschool what other children her age are able to do. Pay attention to how the preschool makes it easier for the children to be successful. For example, children can wash their hands more easily if they have soap and towels in a place they can reach without help. They can put their things away or pick up toys with less assistance if storage places are marked and on low shelves. The more that a child can do on her own, the more competent she will feel, and the more likely she will be to want to be more independent.

Sometimes parents have continued to support habits in their child that are associated with being a baby. Although many three and four year olds have comfort objects such as stuffed animals or special blankets, most children this age are ready to give up the bottles and pacifiers that they know are used by babies, not bigger kids. If your child is attached to a bottle or pacifier, you may want to look at whether having a babylike comfort object is a problem. If your child is in all other ways acting like an independent preschooler, her continued use of the pacifier or bottle may not make a difference. If she seems to think of herself as being little and babylike and is not willing to dress herself or use the potty, she may be ready for you to start treating her more like a child than a baby.

25

REACTING TO A NEW BABY

Everyone told us to expect Charlie to act differently when the new baby arrived, and he did! What was harder to predict was how frustrated we would be with his behavior. Even though we understood his feeling left out and wanting to get our attention when we were busy with the baby, we still got angry with him. When he started to have wetting accidents, I just fell apart. I barely had time to do anything, and now I had a three year old with wet clothes and puddles to clean up.

When a new baby arrives, a family changes in many ways. Before the new baby is born, most parents worry a little about how their older child will feel. They don't want her to feel sad or mad or jealous when the baby is getting her parents' attention. After the baby is born, parents are often less sympathetic and understanding if the older child acts in ways that young children often act when they are sad or mad or jealous. The difference for parents, of course, is that before the baby is born they have time to think about their older child's feelings. After the baby is born, they don't have time to think. If the older child is uncooperative, parents may just get angry.

An older child may be reacting very positively to the baby while acting very negatively toward the parents. This response makes some sense since the parents are the ones who are acting differently: making the older child wait or not picking her up or playing with her when she want them to. The older child's behavior is usually influenced by how she feels about sharing attention and how she thinks she can increase the attention paid to her.

From a child's point of view, her parents can never give her enough time. If she is being asked to share that time with someone else, she will quite reasonably be trying to do things that she believes will get it back. Many children react to a new baby in the family by starting to act like babies. Your child might begin talking baby talk, or wanting a bottle, or needing to carry around a comfort object. Many parents are very upset by this babylike behavior. It's enough work to care for one new baby and a second "baby" is way too much. It can be very tempting to tell an older child, "Stop acting like a baby. You're too old to act that way!"

Telling a child to stop acting like a baby usually doesn't work very well because they are seeing you giving the new baby lots of attention for all of those babylike behaviors. A young child usually makes connections of cause and effect based on what she sees. "The baby wears diapers, cries, sucks on a pacifier, and gets a lot of attention. If I act the way the baby does, then I will get more attention, too."

Having toileting accidents is one of the most common ways for young children to react to the birth of a baby. If a child has been recently trained and was still having a number of accidents at the time the baby was born, it may be easier on everyone to tell the child, "It's too much work for all of us to remember to use the potty right now. You can wear diapers again for a little while and then we'll try again." You can leave the potty chair out so that if your child wants to take herself there without reminders she can, but leave the process up to her. After the new baby is a few months old, you will all have the time and energy to begin again.

If your older child was past the point of frequent accidents, it makes more sense to continue to consider her "trained" and to accept the accidents as a temporary problem. If you make a big fuss or get upset with her, you may wind up with more accidents since she will be getting lots of attention for her behavior. It is best if you can be matter-of-fact about cleaning up and tell her, "Lots of children have accidents when parents are busy or a new baby is taking lots of time." In this way you will be letting your child know that you can understand and accept that her accidents might be related to her feelings, but you are also saying "lots of children" rather than telling your child that you know what she is feeling. She may not be making any connection at all between accidents and her feelings of needing attention, and you don't want to force a connection on her.

Parents can try to encourage a child to stay dry by praising her for remembering to get to the bathroom on time, even if this is behavior that they had been taking for granted a few months earlier. Some children respond well to a chart where a star or sticker marks an accident-free morning or afternoon.

Parents should also try to make time every day to spend alone with the older child. This time is especially important for the mother to schedule, since it is her attention that is usually going to the baby. If a parent spends just fifteen minutes a day with her older child, telling her, "This is our special time, just for us, and someone else will watch the baby while we're together," the effect on the older child's behavior is usually very positive within a few days.

Parents sometimes wonder whether to begin toilet training a child when a new baby is arriving soon. In general, if an older child seems ready and the due date is at least one month away, it makes sense to get started. If you wait, it may be three or four months before your have the energy to begin again, and you will have lost a great deal of practice time. Many children are not distracted from toilet training by the birth of a new baby, and some children even take a giant leap toward becoming trained just to show that they can be more "grown-up" than the new baby!

26

REASONING WITH YOUR PRESCHOOLER

When our son Sam was three, he'd gone on the toilet a few times but then refused to use it. If he couldn't go on his little potty chair, he didn't want to go at all. We finally asked him why he didn't want to use the big toilet. He pointed to a barely noticeable little hairline crack on the seat and said he couldn't use the toilet because of the crack. Well, needless to say, we were convinced that the solution to Sam's refusal was a new toilet seat. It's lucky the crack wasn't on the bowl itself, because after we attached the brand-new seat, Sam still refused to go. We decided to just back off and let him keep using the potty chair. In fact, we even went out and bought another one so that we could take it with us to places that only had big toilets. After a few months, Sam tried using the toilet in our second bathroom one day. That went fine, and within a few weeks he was using whatever toilet or potty was easiest to get to. Before very long, the potty chair was a thing of the past. I'm glad we didn't keep asking him why or we'd probably still be talking about it!

Sam's parents were puzzled and frustrated by his refusal to use the big toilet. They asked him to come up with a reason to explain his reluctance and he did. Once he gave them the reason, they thought that the next step, buying a new toilet seat, would be the solution to the problem, but it wasn't. If they had continued asking Sam "Why?" he might have come up with other reasons, but they guessed that the reasons wouldn't have much to do with how he really felt and that he wouldn't be any closer to using the toilet. Instead of continuing to pressure, persuade, or coax, they let Sam know that was okay to keep using the potty chair until he felt ready to make the switch. They never found out why he was reluctant, but the reluctance diminished with the passage of time.

It is often frustrating for adults when children act in ways that make no sense to us. Adults like to think that if there is a problem, then there must be a solution. They also like to think that what seems logical and connected to a grown-up will be the same way for a child. Haven't we all encouraged a toddler to eat vegetables because they'll make him big and strong, or to go to sleep so that he'll feel well rested in the morning?

So when a young child refuses to use the big toilet, it's natural that parents might first persuade or coax, but if that approach fails, they might ask, "Why don't you want to use the toilet?" Once they ask that question, they may find themselves in the position of Aladdin letting the Genie out of the magic lamp and unable to get him to go back inside. If a child senses that his answer to "Why?" is persuasive enough to make his parents stop nagging him, he may decide to hold on to the explanation even if it was just a spur-of-the-moment thought.

Children can come up with all sorts of explanations to answer a question that begins with "why." Sometimes the answer will be so fanciful that a parent knows that the answer isn't real. If your child tells you he can't eat dinner right now because the knights in his castle are in the middle of a battle, it's pretty easy to stay in his imaginary framework and say, "Let's have the knights on horses take a break so that the horses can get a drink of water while we're having our dinner." With some luck, you can sidestep a confrontation and not have to explain that the knights are just toys and that a make-believe battle can be left until later without disrupting the outcome.

But if parents are feeling anxious or worried about why a child won't do something, and then push their child to justify himself, they may get hooked when a child tells them anything that holds out hope for a solution. Sam's parents thought that a new toilet seat was the solution, so they went out and bought one. They found out very quickly that the explanation wasn't right.

Sometimes a child's answer to a parent's question "Why?" can hook them into even more problems. It's particularly hard if parents ask a child, "Why won't you use the big toilet?" and the child tells his parents that he is afraid. It is true that some children don't like to sit on the edge of a big seat because they feel too wobbly there and some children seem reluctant to watch the toilet flush. Using a child-sized inserted seat or flushing the toilet after the child leaves the bathroom are practical ways of dealing with these problems. It may be that a few children really are afraid that they could fall into the toilet and be flushed away. But the word "afraid" can mean many things to a young child, including "I don't want to and I don't really know why."

Parents who get very anxious about their child's unwillingness to use the toilet can sometimes create more anxiety in the child who doesn't want to be pressured. Most children, if they are afraid of something, will act fearful rather than reluctant. Many will tell their parent that they are afraid without being asked. If a reluctant child discovers that telling his parent that he is afraid seems to persuade them to stop nagging, the child may in fact become more insistent that he is afraid.

This is not to suggest that children are never fearful. Selma Fraiberg, in her wonderful book, *The Magic Years*, talks about the fears that some children may harbor. She describes a four-year-old child who believed that a lobster monster lived in his toilet, and was unwilling to sit there. Fraiberg explains that this little boy had been trying to tell his parents about the lobster monster and they would not listen. The child initiated the discussion, not the parents. Fraiberg did not say that parents must explore a child's fears in order to find an explanation for reluctance to use the toilet!

Anyone who spends time with preschoolers would agree with Fraiberg that children can have fears about everyday activities that seem completely safe to adults. But when children are afraid, they can tell us so without being asked. So when a child has said in words or action, *"No, I don't want to use that big toilet, and I especially don't want to because you keep trying to make me use it!"* it's a good idea to listen, ease up on the pressure, and avoid asking "Why not?"

By providing the child with time to grow taller, bigger, or just more confident, it's likely that you'll watch him make the transition to the toilet without any more of a struggle.

27

WHEN PARENTS DISAGREE

It wasn't until we got to the stage of toilet training that my husband and I started to disagree about what to do as parents. Ryan started to give us a hard time and we weren't sure how much to push him, how much to help, how much to wait. It didn't help that each of us were getting advice from friends and relatives. I couldn't believe that we were actually having arguments about whether Ryan should be wearing training pants!

If two people are trying to do anything together, they will eventually have a conflict or a disagreement. When parents find that they have conflicting ideas about how to care for their child, they should not be surprised. Since there are very few clear-cut right or wrong ways to raise children, it is natural that different people would often have different views. The process of toilet training takes place during a time when children are testing limits, asserting their independence, and requiring a great deal of parental attention in many ways. So a disagreement about the right way to handle a toilet training difficulty is not unusual.

When parents disagree, it is useful for them to look at the disagreement in three ways: What are we disagreeing about? How are we disagreeing? Why are we disagreeing?

- If parents are having different expectations from their child about what it means to be ready for toilet training or what parents should do to help the child along, it may be useful to begin by making sure that each parent's opinion is based on similar information. It will be useful if both parents read the guidelines in this book or talk to the child's healthcare provider to get an idea of what is reasonable to expect or do.

It is usually helpful for parents to find out how their child acts when he is with the other parent, since children often respond differently to each one. What works for one parent may not work for the other, not because one parent is more effective but because the parent–child relationship is different. It is very common for children to test limits more with mothers than with fathers, especially if it is the mother who spends the most time with the child. Once the parents have some agreement about an approach that works for each of them, it is often possible to work out a compromise that respects each parent's point of view. Parents do not have to be completely consistent as long as the child understands what is expected from each parent.

- When parents disagree about how to take care of their child or about anything else, it is important for them to look at how they express and resolve their conflicts. Most parents know that it is not a good idea to have arguments of any kind in front of a young child. Young children cannot judge how angry parents are when voices are raised or the tone is very forceful. They may worry that if their parents are upset they might not be able to take care of the child, or that one parent will leave. It is especially upsetting to the child if parents are arguing about the child's behavior. Then the child believes that he is the source of the problem and that whatever happens to his parents is his fault.

If parents do argue in front of their child, and most parents do at times, they should explain to the child that sometimes parents get angry and disagree, but that the two of you will work it out. It is also important that the child see the parents resolve the issue in words and in the tone of their voices.

- Parents sometimes find themselves disagreeing in many ways about how to care for a child. Sometimes disagreements between parents occur because one parent is feeling as though the other parent is taking too much control of caring for the child. It is common for that parent to feel as though the other is being critical. If a parent feels defensive, it will be hard to work out a solution to a problem. No matter how strongly a parent feels about the wisdom of a certain approach, it doesn't work as well if the other parent is forced into it.

Parents sometimes disagree about how to make rules and set limits with a young child. One parent may think that the other parent is too soft or too hard in discipline. This disagreement may affect toilet training if one parent labels the other as too strict and the other parent says the first parent is too lenient. Parents must take care that toilet training doesn't become a battleground, or a child may react by refusing to go along with either parent's approach.

When parents find themselves in frequent arguments, it can be helpful to join a parent group or to seek professional counseling. Disagreements cannot be avoided, no matter how much parents try. They are a part of family life. Fortunately, it is never too late to learn how to resolve conflicts. Learning to listen to and respect each other's point of view and work out compromises that feel comfortable will help you to be more successful as parents years after the time when your child is toilet trained.

28

MOM'S HOUSE/ DAD'S HOUSE

I f a child is being cared for by parents who are living separately, decisions will have to be made by each parent about what to do when the child is with them. One of the many decisions parents will make together is how to begin and manage toilet training.

It will help if parents are in agreement about what is reasonable to expect from their child. It is also important that neither parent try to pressure the child to be trained faster than she is ready to be. Ideally, each parent will coordinate toilet training plans with the other so the other parent is kept informed about the child's progress. However, it is not necessary for a child to be treated the same by each parent. In fact, a child can be working with one parent on learning to use the potty and be allowed to stay in diapers while she is with the other parent. There are a number of reasons for parents who are living separately to take a flexible approach to toilet training:

- If one parent sees the child less frequently than the other, the parent–child relationship will be different than it is with the primary parent. The child may be more willing to cooperate with the less-seen parent, and less resistant to toilet training activities. At the same time, the child may feel more upset if she has accidents if she is worried about disappointing the parent whom she doesn't see as often.

- It is usually easier for a child to begin learning a new routine in a familiar setting. If a child is moving between two homes, it is possible to begin the toilet training process in one home and to then start up in the other. However, parents can also go over the details of a toilet training plan and agree to have enough similarities in each home for their child to adapt to without much difficulty. It will be more comfortable for the child if there is a potty chair in each home that is similar in size and shape.

- If one parent spends less time with the child and sees her mostly on weekends or in the evening, it may be harder to follow a schedule. If the parent enjoys taking the child out, their activities together will be less disrupted if the child continues the use of diapers during the day until she is having very few accidents.

- Have the child report progress to the other parent by keeping a chart. This is a good way to keep communication open and to give the child a chance to be proud of her accomplishments. Parents will need to agree about what a child needs to do to earn a sticker or star or any other mark on the chart.

- If one parent seems very concerned with the child's toileting achievement and sees it as evidence of better parenting, it is usually a good idea for the other parent to stay out of the competition. Since a child will be more successful in using the toilet when it is her own responsibility, it is better to protect her from any tension between parents.

Children whose parents are separated are no more likely to have difficulties with toilet training than any other group of children. However, all children can be upset by seeing their parents argue and often their distress is expressed through their behavior. If your child is seeming to have difficulties with toilet training or in other ways and you think it may be a reaction to the relationship between her parents, it is a good idea to seek advice from your healthcare provider or a family counselor.

29

BATHROOM LANGUAGE

It's very hard to explain to Billy why it is okay to use the word poop sometimes and not okay other times. I laughed when he said that the mud he tracked in looked like poop, but I didn't think it was funny when he started pointing to other things and called them poop. And it wasn't funny at all when he called his sister a "big pile of poop." But it's hard to explain to a four year old.

A s you have read this book, you may have felt a little uncomfortable at times with the detailed descriptions of toileting activities. Even though the words used throughout the book were chosen to be as neutral as possible, any discussion of the waste products of our bodies and the parts of the bodies involved in producing these wastes tends to make most people feel as though something inappropriate is being said.

In part, this discomfort is probably because the area of the body associated with producing bowel movements and urine is also the area associated with sex. However, our negative reaction is also based on the fact that waste products are not clean and are often unpleasant to smell or see. The words we use can feel unpleasant as well.

The choice of language we use to describe these functions and products is not easy to agree upon, because most people prefer to avoid having conversations using these words. In general, the language we use tends to fall into four categories: the language of adults, the language of children, slang, and "bathroom words."

- The language of adults is the use of words in a way that is biologically correct and generally neutral. In this book, body parts have been referred to using anatomical descriptions and products are referred to as urine and bowel movements. Most of these words are defined in the Glossary because, although they are correct, they are not commonly used or understood. It is a good idea for children to know the correct words for body parts and products even if you do not usually use these words in your family so that they will be familiar with them.

- The language of children is the use of words that are often cute or easy for a young child to say. These words are sometimes the words that were used by parents in their own childhood and may reflect the parents' cultural or ethnic background. If your family uses words that are different from other families you know, make sure that your child understands the other words so that he can get help when he needs to go to the bathroom.

- Slang words are often used by adults to describe toileting activities. They are also often used to express anger or to get a reaction from others. If your child hears you use these words he will without fail repeat them and he too will get a reaction!

- Bathroom words are the words children use to get a reaction from peers and adults. They may be words only used by children, or they may be words that are adult slang. Many children use adult slang not knowing that the words coming from a child can be quite startling. Children figure out very quickly that these words are powerful when used in certain contexts. They also take delight in playing around with words that are all right to use one way, but not all right to use in another. That is why a child will love to talk to his friends using phrases such as "poop head" or "butt face" as well as other words and phrases that are far less amusing. Children often begin to use these words and phrases once they are in preschool because their peers are all thrilled to hear and use bathroom words. Most parents assume that their child learns to speak this way from *other* children!

It will be easier to teach your child to use the words that are acceptable in your family if you already have modeled an appropriate vocabulary and way of speaking. Keep in mind that if you describe body waste as "yucky" or "stinky," you are giving bathroom words an extra emotional charge. It is also helpful if parents do not express anger using highly charged words that they do not want to hear repeated by children. Preschoolers are too young to understand explanations about why adults can use words that they cannot.

When your child uses words that you prefer that he not use, your first step is to tell him that the words that you have heard are not acceptable. "I don't like those words. I know that you are just having fun with them, but we don't talk that way in our family." When you are with a group of children and they begin to buzz with bathroom talk, you can say, "That's not the way I want to hear you talk." Some parents have found that telling a child, "You are a very nice boy, but if people hear you talking that way, they might not know how nice you are." However, you don't have to get into a long explanation of why you are setting these limits. Calm but firm reminders of your rules tend to be effective over time.

If you feel that your child is trying to provoke you with his language, you can ask him to leave the room. Tell him that if he is using language that bothers you or other people, he has to be in his room or somewhere where he can use the words without anyone having to listen to them. If your child is using bathroom words with other children while they play, you may choose to ignore their language if it does not seem to be intended for adults to overhear. Some parents have tried helping their children to figure our substitute words that are silly rather than rude.

The biggest mistake parents make when children use bathroom words is to overreact. Once a young child realizes that he can upset his parents just by saying a word, he is likely to try to shock other people as well. Parents should not use techniques such as washing children's mouths out with soap, putting Tabasco sauce on their tongues, or other harsh punishments to control bathroom language. Even if these methods cause a child to stop using the words around his parents, they are not effective in controlling bathroom language away from home. The resentment that a child may feel from being punished in this way may, in fact, make him more likely to use unacceptable language as he grows older as a way of rebelling against parental control.

30
PRIVACY

Once your child is out of diapers you may notice some changes that go along with her being able to be more in charge of her body. She may be more interested in having privacy when she goes to the bathroom, even if she is not equally interested in respecting other family members' privacy. She may also start to enjoy the freedom to explore her body and to enjoy being unclothed. All of these changes make it necessary for parents to teach a child what is appropriate and inappropriate behavior at home and away from home.

Your child may begin to want to use the bathroom at home by herself. As long as the bathroom is childproofed, her desire for privacy should be respected. Of course, parents should always be alert to noises or the absence of noises that signal to them that their child may be making mischief behind a closed door.

Even if your child is used to bathroom privacy at home, she may have to adapt to less when she is away from home. Most preschools do not allow children complete privacy when using the bathroom, and some expect children to be able to use the toilet in places where other children may be able to watch them. When you are in places away from home where your child cannot be left unsupervised, she will have to be comfortable with an adult staying with her. For these reasons, it is a good idea to allow a moderate amount of privacy at home, but to tell your child that sometimes she has to let a parent come in the bathroom.

Public restrooms pose a problem for young children, especially for little girls when they are out with their fathers. Young children, boys or girls, should not be left alone in public bathrooms. They will need you to help them to cover the toilet seat before using the toilet and to assist them in washing their hands afterward. They will also need your general supervision for safety reasons. Try to scout out the stores and restaurants in your community that make arrangements for children's bathroom use. Try to patronize these businesses and be sure to let the management know you appreciate their consideration. You can also let other businesses know that you think they should provide the same resources.

Once children are out of diapers, they usually love to be naked and to look at their own naked bodies and the bodies of other children. It is common for three or four year olds to cast off all their clothing as casually as an adult takes off his shoes. Your own level of comfort is your best guide to what is appropriate behavior for your child at home. At the same time, it is appropriate for children this age to start learning the difference between family rules and the rules of the outside world. A preschooler should learn that even if she can run around naked at home, she has to keep her clothes on when she goes to the park or to Great-Aunt Mildred's birthday dinner. Parents who did not mind their toddler in the bathroom when they used the toilet usually feel differently if her friends want to come in with her. Over time, children will see many examples of privacy at home and in the outside world and begin to learn what type of behavior is acceptable in different situations.

Your child's interest and delight in her own body will also make her want to explore it further by touching her genitals and by masturbation. Although one and two year olds masturbate, it is not until a child is out of diapers that she can have the freedom to touch herself whenever she wants. Although many parents feel uncomfortable when they see a young child rubbing herself or holding on to himself in a way that is clearly sexual, this behavior is completely normal. However, parents can explain to a child that they understand that it feels good when she touches her private parts, or whatever words parents use to describe genitals, but that it is something that she should do when she is alone. She can be asked to go to her room or save the touching for when she is going to sleep or having a rest. Of course, children cannot be expected to understand the reasons why this activity is restricted any more than they understand many of the other rules that adults impose on them.

This seemingly arbitrary restriction does in fact help children to understand that there are rules and boundaries that most people follow in regard to privacy. It is a good idea for parents to tell their child that now that she is out of diapers, no one else may touch her private parts. It is also a good idea for parents to tell a child that if an older child, a teenager, or an adult ever asks to see or touch her private parts, she should tell her parents or another grown-up. A child who is taught very early about her right to privacy and the importance of telling a grown-up about anyone who violates the rules she has been taught will be much safer.

APPENDIX

QUESTIONS AND ANSWERS

I'm a single mother with a little boy who is just learning how to use the toilet. Should I teach him to stand up to urinate?

It's easier and far less messy when a little boy learns to use the toilet while sitting down. It won't be long before he sees older boys stand up to go. He'll want to try, and that is the time to help him. At that point, you will have to put a stool in front of the toilet so that he will be tall enough and will have to learn to aim. You can help him by placing a sticker in the back of the toilet or by tossing a piece of toilet paper in the water to give him a target. Even with practice, you can expect that it will be quite a while before he doesn't sprinkle the seat and the floor.

My four-year-old daughter wants to stand up to use the toilet the way her brother does. I've tried to explain to her that little girls have to sit down, but she gets angry when I tell her that.

It is probably hard for your daughter to understand why she can't go like a boy, even when you explain. Some children can understand if you tell them that the urine comes out of the body through a tube. A little girl's tube comes out of her body pointing down like a water faucet. A little boy's tube goes through his penis, which can be moved around like a hose in order to aim. If your daughter wants to try, there is no harm in letting her. She will learn more by experimenting on her own than by taking your word for it.

My four-year-old son always wants me to help him wipe himself. Shouldn't he be doing this himself?

You can help your child to be in charge of wiping if you begin by sharing the task with him. First you wipe, then he wipes, and so on. Always have him do the "last wipe." Some children like to check themselves with a mirror. After he finishes wiping, always have him wash his hands.

My daughter wants to wear underpants to preschool, but she still has lots of accidents. The teachers don't mind diapers, but they aren't very tolerant of accidents.

Talk to the teachers about what has worked for other children who are eager to stay dry. They may have some helpful suggestions. Tell your child that it sometimes takes a little while to always remember to get to the bathroom on time. Perhaps she can try to wear underpants for a day or two days. She may be so motivated to wear underpants that she will remember to get to the bathroom in time.

My mother-in-law says that we should give our son a laxative for his occasional constipation. I'm not comfortable with the idea, but does it really cause a problem?

Occasional laxative use is not likely to be harmful, but all laxatives are medicines, even if you can buy them without a prescription. That includes herbal remedies and teas, which can cause cramping. Your child's healthcare provider can advise you best as to whether your child needs a laxative and, if so, which type is safest for your child.

Our two year old loves milk and will often drink four or more glasses a day. I know this makes him constipated but he gets furious when we tell him "no more." What can we do?

It is the nature of a two year old to get furious when a parent says "No!" In this case, your child will be especially angry because you are changing a pattern that was familiar to him. It is usually easier to tell a two year old exactly what a new pattern or rule will be. You can say to him, for example, "From now on, you can have milk three times a day. You can have water or juice at other times." Then, when your child wants more milk, you remind him of the new rule. You can expect him to be angry, but if you just stay calm and don't try to reason with him, he will eventually accept the new pattern.

OTHER RESOURCES AVAILABLE FROM BARRON'S

Butterfield, Moira. *Let's Go Potty.* Hauppauge, NY: Barron's Educational Series, Inc., 2000.

Capucilli, Alyssa Satin. *The Potty Book (for Girls).* Hauppauge, NY: Barron's Educational Series, Inc., 2000.

Capucilli, Alyssa, Satin. *The Potty Book (for Boys).* Hauppauge, NY: Barron's Educational Series, Inc., 2000.

Capucilli, Alyssa, Satin. *Potty Book & Doll (Girls')—Hannah Edition.* Hauppauge, NY: Barron's Educational Series, Inc., 2007.

Capucilli, Alyssa Satin. *Potty Book & Doll (Boys')—Henry Edition.* Hauppauge, NY: Barron's Educational Series, Inc., 2007.

Frankel, Alona. *Once Upon A Potty: The DVD—Her.* Hauppauge, NY: Barron's Educational Series, Inc., 2004.

Frankel, Alona. *Once Upon A Potty: The DVD—Him.* Hauppauge, NY: Barron's Educational Series, Inc., 2004.

Potty Movie DVD, The (Boys') Henry Edition. Produced by Frappé, Inc. Hauppauge, NY: Barron's Educational Series, Inc., 2007.

Potty Movie DVD, The (Girls') Hannah Edition. Produced by Frappé, Inc. Hauppauge, NY: Barron's Educational Series, Inc., 2007.

GLOSSARY

Anal fissure   a small shallow tear in the skin of the anus, usually caused by passing a hard bowel movement. It can be very painful and difficult to heal because of its location.

Anus   the outlet of the rectum lying between the folds of the buttocks.

Constipation   hard or dry bowel movements. Infrequent or irregular soft bowel movements are normal and are not signs of constipation.

Enuresis   the involuntary passing of urine.

Encopresis   the involuntary passing of a bowel movement.

Fiber   the components of plants that cannot be digested and pass through the intestine as part of a bowel movement. Insoluble fiber from the outside layer of wheat and other grains is the most helpful fiber for adding bulk.

Regression   the normal "going backwards" movement of a young child's development.

Temperament   the inborn behavioral style that influences the way a child interacts with caregivers and the environment.

INDEX